The Church on Assignment

W. Eugene Spears, Jr.

BROADMAN PRESS
Nashville, Tennessee

Dedicated to
The Wonderful Churches
with Whom We Have Served Christ

First Baptist Church, Mooresville, NC;
First Baptist Church, North Augusta, SC;
Emerywood Baptist Church, High
Point, NC;
First Baptist Church, Chattanooga, TN;
The Baptist Church of Beaufort, SC

© Copyright 1984 ● Broadman Press
All rights reserved

4250-11

ISBN: 0-8054-5011-4

Unless otherwise indicated all Scripture references are from the King James Version of the Bible.
Passages marked RSV are from are from the Revised Standard Version of the Bible, copyright 1946,
1952, © 1971, 1973. Those marked NASB are from *The New American Standard Bible,* copyright
1960, 1962, 1968, 1971 by the Lockman Foundation. Used by permission.

Dewey Decimal Classification: 262.7
Subject Heading: CHURCH
Library of Congress Catalog Card Number: 84-15541
Printed in the United States of America

Library of Congress Cataloging in Publication Data

Spears, W. Eugene.
  The church on assignment.

  1. Mission of the church. 2. Church. I. Title.
BV601.8.S64 1985   262'.7   84-15541
ISBN 0-8054-5011-4

CONTENTS

Introduction

The purpose of this book is both to chart and challenge the New Testament church in the 1980s. The emphasis is upon the church more as the body of Christ rather than the bride of Christ—the practical instrument, the dynamic congregation—through whom Christ makes his impact upon the world. The "common man" likes to think of himself as "uncommon." The ordinary Christian can become extraordinary when both he and his church become what Christ means for them continually to become. When Mrs. Theron Rankin, wife of the former secretary of my denomination's Foreign Mission Board, was asked about the genius of her late husband she replied simply, "I do not know exactly what to say about him. It is my thought that he was an ordinary man with the world on his heart." Now as never before, we Christians must get the world on our hearts. We must think in terms of world issues; we must pray in terms of world crises; we must give and witness in terms of world needs.

Today when our world is in its greatest turmoil in history, the church of Jesus Christ needs to rediscover her *raison d'etre* so each church can be the church of Jesus Christ and become the body—instrument—through which Christ makes his impact upon the world. In 1 Peter 2:9, Peter used four established Old Testament titles for Israel and related them to the new churches in Asia Minor. The four titles could have been points in one of Peter's sermons concerning the church. Inspired of

God, the apostle Peter declared, "But you are a chosen race, a royal priesthood, a holy nation, God's own people" (RSV).

John McClanahan, in *1 Peter: Message of Encouragement,* writes, "Peter used the Old Testament figures to declare that Christians now were fulfilling Israel's role and vocation. The church was to be the New Israel, with the same kind of calling which had been given to the Old Israel."[1] In the sense that God said to Abram in the first book of the Bible, Genesis 12: "I will bless you, and make your name great, so that you will be a blessing" (v.2, RSV), so now God says to his churches, "I will bless you, I will energize you with my all-powerful Holy Spirit, so that you through your members will be a blessing."

"God's own people" probably refers to the time when God said to Moses and the children of Israel at Sinai, "If you will obey my voice and keep my covenant, you shall be my own possession among all peoples; for all the earth is mine" (Ex. 19:5 RSV).

Today when people are talking about precious stones as being a great investment, we need to realize that God looks upon his Church as a special treasure cherished by her Owner. In a real sense a reining monarch was the owner of everything in his realm, and the kings of that time developed the practice of having some special treasures which were unique as their own cherished possessions. God, who owns all the earth, holds his churches as his prized possessions. As Israel had been called to a witnessing, serving role, so God calls the church today to "declare the wonderful deeds of him who called you out of darkness into his marvelous light" (1 Pet. 2:9, RSV). To discover the depth dimension of being God's people, Christians today need to be humble enough to recognize that we who were once nobodys can now be somebodys in God's forgiving fellowship. Peter declared, "Once you were no people but now you are

God's people; once you had not received mercy but now you have received mercy" (v. 10, RSV). Today the church needs to be and to go forward as God's own people in God's own time to dynamically and creatively carry out God's purpose and God's will!

The writer would like to thank the fellowships of the First Baptist Church of Chattanooga, Tennessee; the First Baptist Church of North Augusta, South Carolina; the Emerywood Baptist Church of High Point, North Carolina; the First Baptist Church Mooresville, North Carolina; and The Baptist Church of Beaufort, South Carolina, for their encouragement and response to these challenges.

He would also like to thank Dr. James Wesberry of Atlanta who loves the church and who encouraged the writing of this book, Dr. Raymond Langlois of Judson Baptist Church, Nashville, and Dr. Charles Page of First Baptist Church, Charlotte, for their encouragement in the ministry for Christ. The writer is indebted to the authors whose books he has read, to the friends who have shared ideas, and to the professors who have inspired him. An effort has been made to give credit where credit is due. No claim is made to originality. The writer has sought to share a vision of Christ's *koinonia,* a church keenly conscious of its sins and shortcomings and passionately striving to know, to be, and to do Christ's mission in the world.

1

The Church Heralds the Primacy of Christ
Luke 18:35-43

In the Holy Scriptures, Greek tragedies, Shakespeare's writings, and modern Broadway offerings, people are fascinated, even mesmerized, by evil. If an author wanted to write a best-seller or create a popular TV series today, he or she would make the main character as mean as possible, as creatively evil as the devil.

R. Z. Sheppard has given a book review on the latest book by Paul Johnson, *Modern Times: the World from the Twenties to the Eighties.* He reported that Johnson suggested: the main problem in our dilapidated and undisciplined world is that Newton's orderly universe has fallen to Einstein's theory of relativity. Einstein never meant to be a Darth Vader; however, Johnson suggested that the social radicals have slipped the idea of relativity into the moral realm, and that moral relativism— the notion that good and evil are matters merely of a point of view—was itself an evil and a disrupting intruder into our ordered world. Johnson suggested that moral relativism is responsible for most of the totalitarianism and terrorism of the past sixty years. The appalling number of murders and other crimes has never even been tallied. At the end of July, 1983, the World Council of Churches met as a "Fellowship of Love in a World of Violence."

Our modern world is inhabited by savagery and violence, and our nation stumbles in the throes of a lack of discipline. The president's Education Commission Report has recently been greeted by cheers and jeers. Bob Teems of Georgetown, South Carolina, relates some excuses received in one of the public school systems: "I'm sorry Tyrone was out, he was sick with a coal." "Deac School; please ackuse John from being absent on January 28, 29, 20, 32, 33." "Chris have an acre in his side." "Mary could not come to school because she was bothered by very close veins." "My son is under the doctor and should not take P.E. Please execute him." "Please excuse Jimmy for being. It was his father's fault."

Our education system may lack some discipline, and our world may feel dislocated and dilapidated, but the people of America are certainly giving prime time and prime consideration to the "Great Galloping Galaxies" and the the struggle and triumph of good over evil.

The May 23, 1983, issue of *Time* magazine devotes a great deal of space to George Lucas and *Star Wars III* or the *Return of the Jedi.* George Lucas's marvelous rocket-propelled fairy tale contains a constellation of special effects, a galaxy of monsters, and a small world inhabited by fierce and furry teddy bears. *Return of the Jedi* was one of the summer of 1983's blockbusters, earning more money on its first day than any other movie in history and forty-one million dollars in its first six days.

Star Wars, the first of the series, has taken in 524 million dollars at box offices around the world. *The Empire Strikes Back,* the second film, had an ending that left the bad guys in charge and the good guys on the run, so it was not as satisfactory. *The Return of the Jedi* completes the trilogy and enables the good guys to conquer decisively and satisfactorily. On the stage of the universe, people enjoy seeing a fight to the death in which the good guys conquer the bad guys, and God triumphs over Satan, but what do the people have in their hearts?

In such a world the church presents the primacy of a fresh,

personal encounter with Jesus Christ, the Lord of the universe, the Son of God, the King of all galaxies in whom the worlds live and move and have their being.

With divine insight and inspiration, the apostle Paul writes excitedly to the Colossians: "And so from the day we heard it, we have not ceased to pray for you, asking that you may be filled with the knowledge of his will in all wisdom and spiritual understanding, to lead a life worthy of the Lord, fully pleasing to him, bearing fruitful in every good work and increasing in the knowledge of God. May you be strengthened with all power, according to his glorious might, for all endurance and patience with joy, giving thanks to the Father, who has qualified us to share in the inheritance of the saints in light. He has delivered us from the dominion of darkness and transferred us to the kingdom of his beloved Son, in whom we have redemption, the forgiveness of sins. He is the image of the invisible God, the first-born of all creation, for in him all things were created, in heaven and on earth, visible and invisible, whether thrones or dominions or principalities or authorities—all things were created through him and for him. He is before all things, and in him all things hold together. He is the head of the body, the church: he is the beginning, the first-born from the dead, that in everything he might be preeminent" (Col. 1:9-18, RSV).

The dynamic church of today recognizes that Christ is the head of the church, the cohesive force for the church, and the preeminent Lord of the universe. The most urgent question therefore that faces each person on this planet is how to confront Christ, how to get right with Christ, and how to commit his or her life to Christ. Samuel Rutherford, the Scotsman who was in prison for his unfailing allegiance to Christ, wrote, "Jesus Christ came into my little cell last night, and every stone flashed like a ruby!" The criterion for judging each worship service of the church is whether or not you have a personal encounter with God in Christ Jesus. You may meet him through the music, the prayers, the Scripture reading, or the message; but whatever the vehicle of communication, you must come face-to-face with Christ.

In this interpersonal encounter, two things always happen: persons gaze into the eyes of Christ and sees themselves as the sinners that they really are, yet they also reads in that face the hope of the persons they can become.[1] The paradoxical prayer of John Hunter becomes their prayer:

> Dear Master, in Whose life I see
> All that I long and fail to be;
> Let Thy clear light for ever shine
> To shame and guide this life of mine.

A creative encounter with God in Christ Jesus will break your heart—and mend it, will stimulate your mind and satisfy it, will turn you off from loneliness and turn you on for a spiritual uplift.

It is not surprising that the God who wrote his Word also honors his Word by giving us an insight into the way to confront his Son. In Luke 18:35-43 we discover a face-to-face encounter with Christ. "And it came to pass, that as he was come nigh unto Jericho, a certain blind man sat by the wayside begging." May I suggest to you that this man is as typical of the latter part of the twentieth century as if he lived around the corner from you—a blind man, begging. The people of the world today have become blind men, begging. Whether they happen to be a Syrian or a Lebanese, an Irishman or an Englishman, an American or a Russian, they seem to be begging for peace but are blind about the avenue to peace. As citizens of the world we have committed the most criminal of all crimes against our fellow human beings—we have substituted the gospel of fear for the gospel of faith. You cannot read the signs of our times in the Middle East, South America, or the United States without realizing that the citizens of the world must choose today between trust or destruction, between faith or annihilation. The only genuine road to peace is through faith in him who is the Prince of peace, Jesus Christ, our Lord! People are not going to beat their swords into plowshares until their hearts beat to the tune of loyalty to Christ. Without any hesitancy, the church of Jesus Christ must arise and declare the primacy and preeminence of Christ over every person's life and the urgency of every person to come and confront this Christ!

Modern man is blind and begging. "And hearing the multitude pass by, he asked what it meant" (v. 36). This question is also being explored today. People are growing more curious, more concerned, more intrigued. "Is the religion of Jesus Christ really different from the religion of secularism? Will Christ be a better God than material possessions and Money Market Accounts? Can Christ give me the spiritual clout that I need to cope with life today? What does Christianity mean for my personal, practical, day-by-day living? Away with your theories and idle illusions—give me the facts!"

"And they told him, that Jesus of Nazareth passeth by" (v. 37). This is exactly what Christianity means: Jesus of Nazareth passes by. The heart of Christianity is a person: Jesus Christ. We believe not so much in a set of rules or a list of abstract ideas but in the historic Son of God. Christianity is not only your relationship to "pie in the sky by and by": it is your growing, dynamic, creative relationship to the living Christ now!

We may not be the most intelligent generation that has ever lived, but we can hear the trumpet blast of all the accumulated lessons of history recorded in 1 John 2:17: "And the world passes away, and the lust of it; but he who does the will of God abides for ever" (RSV). Jesus Christ is the same yesterday, today, forever, and he can transform a person's life today!

What happens when a person confronts Christ? Observe the Scripture: "And he cried, 'Jesus, Son of David, have mercy on me!" (Luke 18:38, RSV). It happened to Peter; it transpired with Thomas; it occurred to Zacchaeus; and it has happened down through the centuries: when a man confronts Christ, he sees himself as he really is, he recognizes his need, and he asks for Christ's mercy and forgiveness.

"And they which went before rebuked him, that he should hold his peace" (v. 39). It has always been the same. When Francis cried out to Christ in the little village of Assisi, Wesley in Britain, Calvin in Switzerland, Luther in Germany, Graham in America—cried for the downfall of superficial, hearsay religion, cried for the upsurge of a vital, firsthand religion—the crowds standing around have always cried: "Stop that voice! Hold your peace! Be quiet! Away with this religious renegade!"

But it took more than the cold shoulder of his friends to keep this man from the Master. The Scripture reads, "But he cried so much the more, Thou son of David, have mercy on me."

Notice the next four words. "So Jesus stood still" (v. 40). The Greek language here means an absolute halt; Jesus stood perfectly still. The Greek language here gives us the picture of a young man marching along the broad highway in the bright sunlight suddenly coming to an absolute halt.

It is important to recall the context of this whole passage. Remember verse 31 above: "Then he took unto him the twelve, and said unto them, Behold, we go up to Jerusalem, and all things that are written by the prophets concerning the Son of man shall be accomplished."

Jesus Christ had set his face as inflexibly as flint to go to Jerusalem. Angry mobs nor jeering crowds, battling armies nor wild beasts, absolutely nothing could stop the Son of God as he marched to Jerusalem to fulfill his divine destiny: nothing, that is, except a poor blind beggar and his personal need.

Here is the heart of hope for people today. It matters not how unworthy we may feel, how searching may be our sins, how perplexing may be our problems, how awful may be our loneliness—*if* we come to Christ in honest faith. The crucial question is not our past thoughts or our past deeds, it is our present faith in Christ!

This particular man was blind, yet he brought his problem to Jesus. Now, of course, the Master could see that the man was blind, but he wanted the man to articulate his faith. Notice that both the request and the answer are very specific: "Jesus stood, and commanded him to be brought unto him: and when he was come near, he asked him, Saying, What wilt thou that I do unto thee? And he said, Lord, that I may receive my sight" (v. 41).

"And Jesus said unto him, Receive thy sight: thy faith hath saved thee. And immediately he received his sight, and followed him, glorifying God: and all the people, when they saw it, gave praise unto God" (vv. 42-43). In our practical age with our practical minds, this is the only practical approach that brings newness of life—a vital faith in Christ that will bring peace to the individual, to the nation, and to the waiting world.

> To worship rightly is to love each other
> Each smile a hymn, each kindly deed a prayer.
> Follow with reverent steps the great example
> Of Christ whose holy work was doing good.
> So shall the wide earth seem our Father's temple,
> Each loving life a psalm of gratitude.
>
> Then shall all shackles fall; the stormy clangor
> Of wild war—music o'er all the earth shall cease;
> Love shall tread out the baleful fire of anger,
> And in its ashes plant the tree of peace!

AUTHOR UNKNOWN

The way to have real peace of mind and heart is to have
forgiveness from God, from other people, and from ourselves.
The need for forgiveness is felt but not perceived today. All too
often it is easy to say, "Forgive us our debts, as we forgive"
(Matt. 6:12), but we act as if we know all about forgiveness and
don't owe any or need a bit of it. Dr. David Redding has
reminded us that forgiveness is free, but it is never free and
easy.[2] Jesus' course on forgiveness is the most advanced He had
to offer; in fact, it is the hardest on the teacher. Before Jesus
acted it all out in the last act on the cross and the resurrection,
he put it into moving words in two businesslike parables.

One night, Simon the Pharisee had Jesus over for dinner. It
appears that Jesus was delighted to attend dispite Simon's half-
hearted invitation. Certainly the Master never wasted his time
with anyone. He put everything he had into everything he did,
and the results were incredible. Simon was the perfect straight
man for the suspense that builds rapidly. While they were
eating dinner, something completely unrehearsed and totally
unexpected shattered the ice of this rigidly puritan household.

In from the streets stepped a fallen woman. She was one of
those who had fallen more than once or twice: it was her whole
life-style. Simon was speechless. Only an Adams in Victorian
Boston could grasp his horror. In the days of Simon the Pharisee the houses opened off the street, and strangers could come
in, go over, sit and talk as long as they kept their place along
the wall. But no woman of the street would dare do such a thing
normally!

Before Simon recovered from the shock of her entrance, she
proceeded to create what to him was a scene. She brought in
an alabaster box, and, suddenly, standing there behind Christ
she broke down into tears. This Jesus was so different from the
others. His eyes were kind and clear. She had never been treated
like that before, and it made her memories more than she could

stand. She took down her hair to hide the red-eyed shame. This would be the night she would never forget, and one that would help her forget the others. She knew it was not wrong because it was holy for her to wash his feet with her kisses and dry them with her hair.

Simon tightened his lips impatiently and tapped his foot all through this part of the scene. The way this Jesus was taking it confirmed his suspicions. If Simon were scandalized by Mary, he was even more disgusted with his guest. "He said to himself, 'If this man were a prophet, he would have known who and what sort of woman this is who is touching him' " (Luke 7:38, RSV). Jesus read his mind clearly and set Simon straight.

Simon had not rolled out the red carpet for Christ in the first place, as was considered common courtesy. The invitation had come out of a dab of curiosity and a pinch of condescension. Jesus did not mind the attitude, but this hostility toward Mary was too much. Here she was, doing the honor Simon had insultingly omitted. Still Simon sneered. Jesus, as usual taking the side of the underdog, came swiftly to her rescue.

"Simon, I have something to say to you." This announcement made Simon perk up with respect, "What is it, Teacher?" (v. 40, RSV).

Mary could not have found a more talented trial lawyer anywhere anytime than Jesus. In a few moments he had developed a case for her defense that Socrates himself could never match. It was this harmless looking little parable here in Luke.

"A certain creditor had two debtors; one owed five hundred denarii, and the other fifty. When they could not pay, he forgave them both. Now which of them will love him more?" (vv. 41-42, RSV).

It was a brilliant stroke. Jesus did not attack Simon. He threw him off guard with the question, then let Simon hang himself. "Which of them will love him most?" Simon had to admit, much as he did not like it, "I suppose that he, to whom he forgave most" (v. 43).

One of the most exciting ideas the world has ever heard was born right then in the mouth of Simon the Pharisee. This does not mean Jesus took Mary's sin lightly. Mary's past was a painful tragedy. Jesus was commending Mary's consciousness of sin, not her sin. The healthy thing about Mary was her guilt feelings which made her eligible for her discovery at the feet of Jesus. She saw what a king's helping of mercy it took to save her life, and it broke her heart with thanks. Which came first, forgiveness or love? Who knows? Love and forgiveness are never very far apart. Love has eyes that can see in the dark. Love has feelings. Love suffers from sin like nothing else. Sooner or later, love learns that it is extremely sensitive to the slightest wish of God.

Simon, orthodox as he was, didn't really care for God: would not cry if God died. Why? First of all, he didn't know about the fall: he didn't realize there was anything wrong with himself. "For all have sinned, and come short of the glory" (Rom. 3:23) was news to him. Simon couldn't think of a thing to apologize for, couldn't think of a thing God would need to forgive him for; so since he thought he didn't need mercy, he thought he didn't need the God of mercy. Simon was unconscious of his own evil, so he was unsaved, unloving, lost!

Sin presents two faces. Sometimes sin is something you do: Mary did that. But sin can keep you from doing something: Simon's brand of sin. Mary's heart was rank with weeds, but Simon's heart was stone cold. Jesus introduced Simon to himself that night remorselessly by comparing the way he had not acted to the way Mary did act. Mary was moved to do something; Simon's hardened hands stood still.

It was getting late, so Jesus spoke roughly to raise Simon from the dead. "Do you see this woman? I entered your house, you gave me no water for my feet, but she has wet my feet with her tears and wiped them with her hair. You gave me no kiss, but from the time I came in she has not ceased to kiss my feet. You did not anoint my head with oil, but she has anointed my feet with ointment. Therefore I tell you, her sins, which are many, are forgiven, for she loved much; but he who is forgiven little, loves little" (vv. 44-47, RSV).

The second parable Jesus presented was said in answer to another kind of Simon: "Lord, how often shall my brother sin against me, and I forgive him? As many as seven times?" (Matt. 18:21, RSV).

Jesus replied, "I say not unto thee, Until seven times: but, Until seventy times seven" (v. 22, KJV). Simon said seven times to be big about it since the law asked for only three. But Jesus said seventy times seven, not to make it complicated but to carry it out to infinity, to make sure that Simon saw that the maximum mercy of which a man is capable is microscopically small compared to the mercy God has given us.

This second parable introduces us to a man in high position of responsibility near the king. After an auditing, it was discovered that he had taken ten thousand talents from the king's treasury—a tremendous sum. The total annual taxes of Judea, Idumea, Samaria, Galilee, and Perea, all together, amounted to only eight hundred talents. The king's prime minister had embezzled about two million dollars, and that would have created a scandal even in Saudi Arabia or Iran or Lebanon today. The king, naturally alarmed at such flagrant dishonesty, "commanded him to be sold, and his wife, and his children, and all that he had, and payment to be made. The servant therefore fell down and worshipped him, saying, 'Lord, have patience with me, and I will pay thee all.' The lord of that servant was moved with compassion, and loosed him, and forgave him the debt" (Matt. 18:23-27).

Look closely, my friend, doesn't that debtor look familiar? This was not an allegory but a situation that is the perfect likeness to ours: human, full of faults—we are precisely in the same predicament as this man, fallen into the swirling sea of many mistakes. We have sinned in number as the sands and are no longer worthy to be called "thy children." But God in his mercy has pardoned us.

It took a cross to bring us back to life. The better the person, the better he can see what is wrong with him. The first sign of a saint is this highly developed sense of sin. The Pharisee held his head high because he was not like other men. The saint hung his head low because he was not like Christ. "Nowhere," cried Saint Francis, "is there a greater, more miserable, poorer sinner than am I!"

After the blazing light of forgiveness, the stage was plunged into darkness. The forgiven prime minister was seen meeting his servant who owed him a little money. Compared to what the prime minister owed the king, it amounted to nothing. The prime minister ordered the poor fellow to pay up immediately. The man fell at his fellow servant's feet and begged him, "Have patience with me, and I will pay you" (v. 29), but he refused and had him jailed until he should pay the debt. When the prime minister's colleagues saw what he had done, they took it to the king. When the king heard it, he was enraged and ordered the prime minister back into his presence, storming, "I forgave you all that debt because you besought me; and should not you have had mercy on your fellow servant, as I had mercy on you?" (vv. 32-33, RSV). The king made him take his own medicine and sent him to prison. Then Jesus said those terrifying words, "So also my heavenly Father will do to every one of you, if you do not forgive your brother from your heart" (v. 35, RSV).

God was not vindictive: this was simply the parable's way of shouting that forgiveness was a matter of life and death! God gave and forgave in this way!

Forgiveness won't work until it flows from one to another. A person who can't give mercy can't understand how to get it. God's forgiveness cannot flow in upon the imprisoned soul until the doors are opened out to show mercy to another person. The sentence we shall receive when we stand trial after death will be the verdict we gave our brother back in the jury box of life.

Kenyan J. Scudder, one of the great prison wardens of the West, often told about the time when a friend of his was on a train and noticed that the young man sitting next to him was feeling very low. The young man confessed that he was a convict just released from a penitentiary. His whole life had cast such a dark shadow over his family, and they had felt such shame that he had lost all contact with them.

He kept hoping against hope, however, that they had forgiven him, and that the almost dead silence of many years meant that they were too poor or too ill to write. So before his prison sentence was up, he had devised this plan to find out how they felt. He wrote a letter home explaining that he would be on the train that passed their little farm on the outskirts of town. If they could forgive him, they were to hang a white ribbon on the old apple tree near the tracks. If it were not hanging there when he came by, he would not bother them ever again. As the train approached the familiar landmarks of his boyhood days, the suspense became more than he could bear, and he changed seats with his companion, asking him to look out the window for him. In a minute the tree was in sight and with eyes bright with sudden tears, his companion placed his hand on his knee and whispered hoarsely, "It's alright, boy! The whole tree is white with ribbons!"[3]

Here in the mid 1980s, we need to recognize that we are all on death row until we decorate our trees like that. "If ye forgive

men their trespasses, your heavenly Father will also forgive
you" (Matt. 6:14). An undisciplined and dilapidated world is
hungry today to hear that King Christ can and will forgive, and
that receiving Christ's forgiveness even we, too, can learn to
forgive and be free.

2

The Church Ministers to the Total Person
John 2:18-25

Not long ago Paul Harvey told about a young couple who drove up to a drive-in theater in Chicago. The ticket salesman explained, "We'll be glad to have you come in and see our movie, but if your baby there on the seat with you cries, you'll have to leave."

They drove on to the gate and the ticket collector explained, "You can go in and see our movie, but if your baby cries you'll have to leave. We will refund your money, but if your baby cries you'll have to go."

The young couple drove on in, got situated, and saw about a third of the picture. The husband turned to his wife and asked, "What do you think of the movie?"

The wife responded with indignation, "This picture is awful! It's the worst movie I ever saw!"

Then the husband instructed, "OK, Ethel, reach over and pinch the baby!"

We smile because of the surprising end to this story. Just getting a partial glimpse of a situation or a person and assuming that this impression tells the whole story is not only unfair, it is also inaccurate.

Time magazine called Jacques Ellul's book *The Meaning of the City,* "The year's most important theological work." Ellul asked whether a Christian can justify being a part of the inhuman, fragmented, modern metropolis; but we in the church believe that this issue is not debatable. We are an integral part of our world whether we want to be or not, and Christ calls us to be his dynamic fellowship to reach out and redeem the people of our world. This is the name of the game; this is where the action is—to pray, to give, to go, and to reach people in our world for Christ!

The relevant question is: How do we look upon people today? In a profound sense, do we see people through the eyes of Christ? Are we moved by the compassion and concern of Christ to reach out to people?

We can say for certain that on every page of the Word of life we are taught that we must never look upon people as though the first glance told the whole story. Labels may help in a supermarket or a department store, but labels should never be used on people. When you work with people and seek to help people, labels are really a hindrance. Ronald Sleeth pointed out that labels block communication.[1] The merits of a person's ideas are dropped immediately if you can paste a certain label on them. A friendly discussion comes to a screeching halt when someone drops the phrase, "Isn't that the approach of a radical liberal?" Or "Isn't that what a homosexual said in San Francisco?" No one wants to be stigmatized, so communication is stopped. The subject under discussion becomes taboo, and the people remain strangers.

Labels not only block communication, they also stop our thinking. A label represents a conclusion, so what more is there to consider? In the city of Chicago, a radio program is called, "Candid Microphone." Questions are asked people on the street, and a concealed microphone picks up their comments. One afternoon, the announcer stood in front of the Marshall Field Department Store and whispered confidentially to the people about to enter, "Have you heard that this building is retroactive?"

Perhaps only Marshall Field could have stood the experiment; because many, many shoppers quickly changed their course and went to another store . . . "That building was retroactive."

Before a person smiles too easily, he should remember when he bought toothpaste because it had a "a special, sexy brightener" or hair tonic because it contained "the miracle ingredient of lanolin" or face cream because it boasted of having "NPQUZ 33, as opposed to 32 or 34." The person bought these articles without having the foggiest clue as to what these "miracles" really meant.

Labels block communication, impede a person's thinking, and, they tend to force a person into an either/or position. They become halos or stigmata—no middle way. Politically, a label forces a person to be either a liberal or a conservative; religiously, a fundamentalist or a liberal; socially, an old, old fogy or a "cool, cool dude." People are not absolutely and always those kinds of animals—they act one way one time and another way another time. To say that a person is always an "old fogy" is not only unfair, it is also inaccurate. It isn't true or factual.

Fourth, labels are dangerous because they trigger a person's emotions and cloud his brain. Many times a friendly discussion of politics comes to a screeching halt when one man exclaims, "You're a liberal!" and another shouts, "You're a conservative!" Two men, perfectly rational one minute, become emotional fanatics the next moment.

It is dangerous, unfair, and inaccurate for any member of a church to put a label on another person. We must learn to consider each individual not as a position or a point of view but as a person, a whole universe within himself or herself. The heart of the New Testament church is that we must keep the lines of communication open; we must keep on thinking and reasoning; we must not force people into an either-or position, and we must not allow our emotions to strangle our mature judgment.

This discussion leads us to an important Scripture text that needs to be considered in these days. Two verses can be closely connected. One of the most penetrating and revealing messages in the Bible is John 2:24-25, "Jesus did not commit himself unto them, because he knew all men, And needed not that any should testify of man: for he knew what was in man." He who created us knows the faults, the frailties, the foibles of every person. Christ understands our fondest dreams and our deepest desires. He knows what makes us tick and what can make us click, and this wonderful Christ gives the key to the finest Christian relationships and the key to an individual spiritual growth program when he says, "A new commandment I give unto you, That ye love one another; as I have loved you, . . . By this shall all men know that ye are my disciples, if ye have love one to another."

In these critical days through which we are passing Christ says that we are not to treat people as a position or as a point of view but as a person, an interesting person with needs and rights and dreams. We are to see each person as Christ sees that person—a whole universe with unlimited possibilities, and we are to love those persons as Christ loves them by helping them to have a spiritual encounter with Christ.

Two Scotsmen, one the head of the chemistry department at the University of Edinburgh and the other an author on a secluded Pacific Island, have a similar suggestion. Dr. Henry Drummond declared, "The church is a society of the best people working for the best ends, according to the best methods. Its law is one word: loyalty, and its gospel is one message: love."

Robert Louis Stevenson prayed, "Lord, give us the strength to encounter that which is to come, that we may be brave in peril, constant in tribulation, . . . and down to the gates of death, loyal and loving one to another."

No, the New Testament church which we seek to be is not a perfect organism because it is composed of imperfect people. But as we endeavor to reach people for Christ, which is our biblical imperative, as we yearn to be a relevant church in a fragmented and lonely world, as we strive to grow and expand each fellowship, we must resolve to lay aside all labels and to love people as Christ loves them.

A certain daughter's father carried the label of a "drunkard." So abominable and abusive was he that the girl had to leave home. Then one day she joined a Sunday School class, and there she heard about the love of Jesus. She learned that though people snubbed Christ, he still sought to win them; though they crucified him, he loved them enough to lay down his life to save them, and Joanie's heart was so moved she became a Christian.

"Now," she said, "I must go back home and help my father."

"But Joanie," argued a friend, "he's a drunkard! What will you do when he finds fault with all your efforts to please him?"

"I'll just try a little more," she answered with a soft light in her eyes.

"Yes, but when he's unreasonable and unkind, you'll be tempted to lose your temper and answer him angrily! How will you handle that?"

"I'll just pray a little more," she replied with determination.

"But Joanie, suppose he should slap you around as he did before, surely you'd leave him!"

"No," she smiled, "I'll just love him a little more."

You do not have to guess the climax of this story. Joanie's father's life was transformed, and he became a Christian because she loved him a little more with a love like the love of Christ!

If there is one word which can describe and discipline Christians this year, it is the word *responsible*. We must be responsible to Christ. In the most critical time of their discipleship, Jesus came to his followers and said, "All authority in heaven and on earth has been given to me. Go therefore and make disciples of all nations, . . . and lo, I am with you always, to the close of the world" (Matt. 28:19-20, RSV).

At the beginning of his public ministry, we read, "When [Jesus] saw the crowds, he had compassion on them, because they were harassed and helpless, like sheep without a shepherd" (Matt. 9:36, RSV). Christ was always moved by the multitudes, and he challenges us to be motivated to lead the multitudes to him and through him to the life that is worth living today.

The National Broadcasting Company recently presented a three and one-half hour television special on violence in America. What Americans saw was ugly, painful, and alarming. Our crime rate has risen steadily and shows no sign of decreasing. Nashville, Tennessee, in 1982 reported that the preceding year had a decline in the crime rate, but it is perhaps the only major city to make that boast. We hear reasons enough for widespread crimes, such as broken families, ghettos, below-level education and housing, yet the Watergate crowd had good jobs and fine houses. Much of the crime in America in the 1980s is committed by the well-fed, well-clothed, well-entertained, well-employed people. People steal, not because they are poor, but because they are *sinners*. People kill, not because they do not have good houses, but because they do not have *good hearts*.

The number of unmarried couples living together has increased 102 percent since 1970, and the rise in illegitimate births has gone up from 5.3 percent to 14.3 percent! Today as never before we need to make it clear that the church of Jesus Christ does not condone cohabitation before marriage or approve pornography in the home or anywhere else! Immorality with the pill or without the pill will break one's life and shatter one's chances for the future. Just before he left office, President Jimmy Carter stated, "The breakdown of the American family has reached extremely dangerous proportions. There can be no more urgent priority for our administration than to see that every decision our government makes is designed to support and strengthen the American family!"

Today as never before we must rediscover the motivation that Christ has for each Christian. Someone asked John Dillinger how he would motivate people, and Dillinger replied, "Just put a forty-five on his chest and tell him what to do!" But there are other ways to motivate people.

Once a young fellow was warned not to cut across a certain pasture. One day he decided to try it and, surely enough, a 2500-pound bull got after him. He ran and ran and leaped to reach a limb that was ten-feet high; he missed it, but he caught it on the way down!

Seriously, every city in America has a distinctive beauty: dedicated and gracious people, but it also has lost and lonely people who need to be led to Jesus Christ. Between 11:00 AM today and 11:45 AM tomorrow, 146,000 people will die in our world, and the majority of them have never heard of Jesus Christ. The motivation we must recognize today comes from five directions: the first is from above from the heart of God.

The apostle John exclaimed, "Herein is love, not that we loved God, but that he loved us, and sent his Son to be the propitiation for our sins" (1 John 4:10). When we realize that the call to set people free comes from God, not from us, then we gain freedom from the present frantic frustration of life—the present freeway kind of living, and we begin to realize that we are responsible instruments in the hand of God! It is God who calls us to deliver this world and to set people free for the glory of God and the good of humanity!

Second, our motivation comes from beneath! The Bible

makes it clear that there is a hell; and we are to recognize it, believe in it, and seek to help people avoid going there. The Bible says plainly in the Book of Romans that sin pays off: "The wages of sin is death" (6:23). In the vivid story of Lazarus and Dives, the Bible said that Dives lifted up his eyes from hell— burning, painful, excruciating torment.

Our motivation comes from above from God; it comes from beneath from the danger of hell, and, third, our motivation comes from without from the people who are hungry and hurting and who need to know Christ as their Savior, Lord, and loving Friend. Back in Queen Anne's time in England there were no street lights. Even such a huge, sprawling city as London became totally dark when the sun went down. It therefore became necessary for each home to let its light shine, even to hang out a lantern near the door of the house so that pedestrians could find their way. If even one home failed to show its light, people would stumble and fall in the darkness.

Do we in the 1980s really believe that a person outside of Christ is lost for today and lost for eternity? Do we really believe that a person outside of Christ will go to an eternal torment? Do we really believe that God calls each Christian who has received the light of Christ to share that light today? Then surely we are compelled by the compassionate love of Christ to go to the people outside, those without Jesus, and lead them to the One who is the way, the truth, and the life!

Many times it has been our privilege to hear the old adage: to understand is to forgive. Understanding is like electricity; potentially, it is one of the most powerful forces in human life, but it must be used to be effective. How wonderful we all feel when we think another person understands our problems or shares our concerns. Shared sympathy for another person can change a whole day into sunshine and the longest path into a song.

Have you heard of the tragic plight of Bozo, the circus elephant? Beloved of all the children Bozo had been a well-valued animal for several years. In the center of the ring he waltzed and pirouetted, lay down, and played dead, and at the grand finale he led the parade with an American flag in his trunk.

But no more! Three times within a week he had tried to kill his keeper. He had roared at boys and girls with peanuts as if he would like to trample them. It seemed that nothing could calm him down, and finally the authorities told his owner that Bozo must be put to death. He was a public menace. The manager thought there might be a chance to make up his losses, so he sold a tremendous number of tickets to the elephant's execution.

Rapidly, the news rushed along the city streets, and huge crowds turned out to witness the spectacle. As they entered the main tent on Saturday morning they beheld a large pile of army rifles stacked and ready. Beside the rifles waited a squad of gunners. Bozo trudged around a never-ending circle, and often he lifted his trunk to bellow at the crowds. It was almost as if he suspected the coming events. In his shiny top hat and coat, the ringmaster prepared to give the signal to begin the execution.

Suddenly he felt a strong hand on his shoulder. To his surprise, he discovered a short, stocky man with thick-lensed glasses and a brown derby hat. "Do you really want to kill that elephant?" asked the stranger. "Wouldn't you rather keep him alive?"

"Of course, I would, but there is no chance. He has become a dangerous elephant, and the authorities have asked me to destroy him. Bozo must die."

"Would you mind if I tried to make him well? Just give me two minutes in the cage, and I'll guarantee his safety."

The manager looked wistfully at this brown-moustached

stranger. But no! To enter that cage would mean certain death. "Why, you'd be mincemeat in a matter of seconds! I couldn't possibly let you do it!"

"I thought you'd say that," grinned the little man; "therefore, I have brought a legal release for you. All the risk will be mine." Being assured that the document was authentic, the manager turned and broke the sensational news to the crowds. Never before had there been a show like this!

Briskly the little man removed his hat and coat. "Now," he said calmly, "you may open the door."

At the rattle of the lock, Bozo halted in his incessant prowl and turned bloodshot eyes toward the steel door. He gave a warning squeal of wrath, but unarmed, the intruder stood his ground. Softly, he began to speak. Hearing the first words, the elephant became strangely quiet. The tent's audience could clearly hear the man speak, but they couldn't understand a single word. Only Bozo seemed to understand the language. After hearing the first words, the elephant quieted down.

Presently, everybody heard a new cry, a small cry from a dangerous animal, now childlike and piteous. The enormous head began to wag from side to side. It was as if Bozo were overpowered by something beautiful and beloved. Now the little man ventured nearer. He lifted his hand and patted the trunk. Then, with the end of it curled around his wrist, he began slowly to promenade with the elephant round and round the cage. At last, the astonished audience could bear the sight no longer, and they burst into cheers of rapture!

As the little man left the cage he said to the manager, "There was nothing bad about Bozo. He was just homesick. He's an Indian elephant, and I talked to him in Hindustani, the language he grew up with. It sort of made him feel at peace again, and he'll be all right for a long time."

The man disappeared before the manager could thank him,

but glancing at the piece of paper left behind he stared twice at the signature, then a new light began to dawn. The stranger's name was Rudyard Kipling.

It is the understanding heart that makes all the difference. The person who most revealed this healing heart was not the famous writer Rudyard Kipling or the famous physician William Mayo but the famous Son of God, Jesus Christ.

In a fascinating incident we see the Master as he penetrated the problem and purged the problem of the woman caught in sin. Being very weary from his journey through Samaria, Jesus paused at Jacob's well. A woman came to draw water, and Christ asked for a drink. "How is it that you being a Jew request water from a Samaritan woman? Jews have no dealings with Samaritans!"

Jesus answered, "Every one who drinks of this water shall thirst again, but whoever drinks of the water that I shall give him will never thirst; the water that I shall give him will become in him a spring of water welling up to eternal life" (John 10:13-14, RSV).

Naturally, the woman said, "Sir, give me this water, that I may not thirst, nor come back to draw" (v. 15, RSV).

Having aroused her curiosity, Christ penetrated the core of her problem with his keen understanding. "Go, call your husband, and come back to me."

"I have no husband," confessed the woman (v. 17).

"That's true. You have had five husbands, and the man you have now is not your husband."

How often have people felt that they could hide their sins! Briefly, temporarily, they may succeed in keeping their wrongs from other people, but they can never hide them from God. No amount of feverish activity or glossy paint or mental excuses will cover up their wickedness. With his understanding heart,

Jesus searches their lives and penetrates the core of their problems.

But what if the story stopped there? People caught, trembling, fearful, with their sins displayed before the all-seeing eyes of God. It is a picture to drive them mad! But thanks be unto God the Christian symphony does not end on this somber note of judgment. First, there comes the crashing chords of justice, then the lilting lyrics of joy.

With her sins clearly understood by Christ, this woman frantically sought a refuge. "Uh, you must be a prophet. I know that when the Messiah comes he will tell us all things." Then Jesus brought the only real remedy for her need. He both penetrated and purged her problem by saying, "I that speak unto thee am he" (v. 26).

This is the good news of the gospel! A person no longer needs to cringe and collapse under the weight of sin with the piercing eyes of the holy God penetrating his heart. There was another cross that stood all alone on a lonely hill outside Jerusalem. On that other cross, the sins that a person now suffers were the nails, the thorns, and the spears that crucified the Son of God. Once and for all, Jesus paid the penalty for our wrongs. If persons will confess their sins to him, they can walk away with refreshing joy in their hearts. They can sing, "I have met the Christ with the understanding heart. He penetrated my problem and purged that problem out of my life. Come and see this fair, forgiving, freedom-giving Christ!"

Our motivation comes from above—from the heart of God to the hungry and hurting hearts of people, from beneath—from the reality and dangers of hell, from without—from the longing souls of lost people who need to learn and to give their lives to Jesus, and, fourth, from within each Christian. Andrew Carnegie, who built an empire in steel, said, "If you take everything I have away except my people, I could build it all again.

My people make all the difference!" Christians in the 1980s are literally the people of Christ, called by our Master to go out and share our Christ.

As soon as Andrew found Christ, he immediately went to find his brother, Peter, to lead him to Christ! As soon as Phillip found Christ, he immediately went to find his brother, Nathaniel, to lead him to Christ! The biography of Dwight L. Moody, the great evangelist who led hundreds of people to Jesus, was appropriately called *The Borrowed Glow.* God calls our churches today not to be a sacred society to snub sinners, but to be a golden flame with the spiritual glow that leads people to Christ! We who have received the light of Christ, we who have felt the warm glow of Christ's love, we are called from within our hearts and our minds and our souls to share that love.

When John Newport was the pastor of a small rural church, the church had a revival one week. One night the evangelist asked the congregation of people which was already standing to walk over and stand by the persons who led them to Christ. There was a humble lady in the congregation who was not at all successful in terms of the world's standards, yet over half the congregation walked over and stood by her.

Finally, we are motivated by the resurrected Christ. In Revelation 3 the victorious Christ invites, "Behold, I stand at the door and knock; if any one hears my voice and opens the door, I will come in to him and eat with him, and he with me. He who conquers, I will grant him to sit with me on my throne, as I myself conquered and sat down with my Father on his throne. He who has an ear, let him hear what the Spirit says to the churches" (vv. 20-22, RSV).

When Holman Hunt painted the touching picture of Jesus at the door, a friend commented, "You made a mistake, you left the knob off the door!" Hunt replied, "No, the knob is on the inside. If we open the door, the eternal Christ will come in and will warm our hearts, recreate our souls, and give us newness of life!"

In his very down-to-earth book on psychiatry, Karl Menninger reminded us that it is the beginning of mental health to realize that life is a struggle. Every person experiences the paradoxical tension that exists between taking care of his rights and doing his duty, between looking out for number one and looking out for his neighbors, between being in the world and yet not being a part of the world. Today in the 1980s we say very glibly, "Life is hard by the yard, but by the inch, it's a cinch." The fact is that life for many people is hard by the yard and by the inch.

We are glad that when the apostle Paul presented the analogy of the Christian dying to the old man and being born to the new man, he used the present tense to show that this is a continuous action (Rom. 6:6-8), not a point action. The real Christian is continually dying to the old man and continually striving to become the new man in Christ. Somehow we must discover a master motive that will moderate our desires and defeats and carry us surely and safely through. The Gospel of to John gives us that master motive in the *resurrected Christ.*

Perhaps most important of all, the living Christ has the power to change a person's despair into hope. A Scottish preacher was giving a sermon on profanity, making this statement: "If I were making a list of the most profane words in the English language, I would leave out a lot of slang that shows more naïvete and stupidity than wickedness, but the first and most profane word I would list is the word *hopeless.* When you say a person or a thing is hopeless, you are even denying the God who brought Jesus Christ up from the dead!"

When Dante in his *Divine Comedy* wanted to picture the awfulness, the terror of going to Hades, he sought a slogan to carve over the gate of hell. What did Dante write? "All who

enter here will burn in eternal fire forever"? No. Did he say,
"All who enter here must abandon their loved ones forever"?
No. Over the gate leading into Hades, the most frightening
thing that Dante could imagine was: "Abandon hope, all ye
who enter here!"

In the long ago two disciples on the road to Emmaus were
filled with despair. They began to exclaim to the stranger,
"When Christ was alive he filled us with such hope! He said the
kingdom of God was at hand! We hoped it was he who would
redeem Israel! But now he's dead on a cross!"

Certainly Mary Magdelene was not really hoping for Christ's
resurrection. When the stranger came to her there in the garden, she referred to his dead body when she exclaimed, "They
have taken away my Lord, and I know not where they have laid
him" (John 20:13).

Thomas thought the cause was so hopeless that he didn't
even stay with the other apostles. He said to them, "Unless I
shall see in his hands the imprint of the nails and put my finger
into the place of the nails, and put my hand into His side I will
not believe" (v. 25, NASB). Thomas was not even there when
Christ first appeared to his apostles.

Then God changed their hopeless despair into an eternal
hope! Christ was not tricked, Christ was not trapped, Christ
was triumphant when he was crucified and arose from the dead!
Yes, the beauty of Christmas, the glory of Palm Sunday, the
sacredness of Good Friday would be as nothing if it were not
for the fact that Christ rose on Easter morn! Historians tell us
that the resurrection of Jesus Christ is "the best-attested fact in
history," but much more important than this documentation,
the resurrection of Jesus Christ is proven by the lives that were
transformed in his presence!

The two men on the road to Emmaus suddenly recognized
the living Christ, and their despair was changed to hope. "He

set our hearts ablaze!" they cried. When Mary Magdelene saw
and knew that this stranger in the garden was none other than
her risen Lord, joy unspeakable flooded her trembling soul!
When old doubting, despairing Thomas came face-to-face with
the risen, triumphant Christ, he didn't even mention proof. He
didn't thrust his hand into Jesus' side or put his fingers into the
nailprints in Jesus' hands. Instead, Thomas fell to his knees and
cried, "My Lord and my God" (v. 28).

Take a closer look at Simon Peter. If the curtain had gone
down on Peter at Calvary, his life would have been almost as
shameful as Judas's. Peter had denied Christ three times in one
night. Still there was hope for a man like Peter. In a heartwarm-
ing way, the angel said, "Go tell his disciples and Peter that
Christ has risen!" (see Mark 16:7). Don't leave old Simon Peter
out. So Simon Peter became a conquering witness of the resurrected riches of God in Christ Jesus.

What about the apostle Paul? So far as we know, Paul had
no personal contact with Christ "in the days of his flesh" (Heb.
5:7). Saul was bitterly persecuting this "new way" in religion.
With all of his pharisaical and scientific background, Saul
would have been the first to denounce any trace of magic or
superstition. But one day on the Damascus road, Saul met not
a memory, not a vague ghost; Saul met the risen Christ! And
in Christ's presence, Paul could learn to "do all things through
Christ" who strengthened him (Phil. 4:13).

Today this resurrected, living Christ goes on conquering and
to conquer. You and I meet not just a memory enshrined in a
sacred Book but the risen, triumphant Christ today! In his
presence our convictions are moved to the commitment of the
whole of our lives! The master motive of our being is that we
can walk and talk and live and *share* our Savior, our Inspiration, our Shepherd, our Lord!

Take another look at the close of John's Gospel. After the

mountaintop experience of the resurrection, the disciples came right back into the valley of the common tasks of life. They had the prosaic job of providing food. Peter said, "Men, I'm going fishing," and the others went along. They sought all night and caught nothing, but when the risen Christ told them to cast their nets on the other side they caught so many fish their nets almost broke! As they beached their little boats, they saw that their risen Lord had breakfast ready for them. He had cooked a little bread and a few fish, and it was all prepared for his tired and hungry disciples. By so doing he who is the Bread of life taught his disciples that he would always be their Savior and Shepherd for the whole of life, for the mountaintops as well as for the valleys.

The last words that John recorded of Jesus were, "Follow thou me" (21:22). Thus, with Jesus and his little band of disciples finishing breakfast on a sandy beach, one of the greatest of all the Gospels comes to a close. Is it anticlimactic? By no means. The gospel began with the cosmic picture of the living Word who was with God before the world began. Yes, this is the close of Christ's days on earth in the flesh, but this is certainly not the end of the story. This is merely the close of the chapter and the beginning of a new chapter that Christ calls even greater than the last. This is the beginning of that chapter on world conquest. The risen Christ invites these disciples to follow him; on and on down through the centuries, he is continuing to invite, "Come, follow me," and we today can hear his call. We have the glorious opportunity of working, witnessing, doing our best to lead others to join our happy throng until that day when the kingdoms of this world shall become the kingdoms of our Lord and of his Christ, and he shall reign forever!

Twelve miles north of Chicago stands Northwestern University at Evanston. Years ago two farm boys came to the college from Iowa, Will and Edward Spencer. Ed was a strong swimmer.

On the morning of September 8, 1860, word reached the college that a steamer was wrecked off Winnetka, Illinois, on Lake Michigan. A crowd of students, including the Spencer brothers, rushed to the scene of the wreck. When they arrived, the steamer *Lady Elgin* was going to pieces, but a number of passengers were still afloat.

Ed Spencer plunged into the lake, again and again saving men, women, and children. Each time as he would succumb to the cold and exhaustion, his companions would plead for him not to try again, that he himself would be drowned. But he persisted, swimming through heavy waves sixteen times and rescuing seventeen persons in all.

At last they pulled him from the angry waters. Tender hands lifted him from the beach and carried him back to the college. All that night in the college dormitory he moaned, "Did I do my best?" The bronze memorial tablet at Northwestern University closes its statement of his heroic deed with his often-repeated question: "Did I do my best?"

Today church members stand beside the stormy seas of the 1980s. Human wrecks are everywhere: men and women going down to destruction, but as Dr. George Truett often put it, "If we abide in Christ, we will abound in Christ." If we give our lives to this resurrected Christ and do our best for the Master, then the risen Christ will be our motivating power and will transform our lives.

The church with the understanding heart is moved to see each person as a whole universe, warts and all, and is energized by the risen Christ to share his redemptive love.

Certainly there are many unloved and lonely people in our world today. How does a Christlike congregation meet their real needs?

3

The Christlike Congregation Touches the Hearts of the Unloved and the Lonely

Colossians 3:9-17

Dwight L. Moody is credited with the statement, "There is one thing I have noticed as I have traveled in different countries. I have never known the Spirit of the Lord to work where the people are divided. There is one thing that we must have if we are to have the Holy Spirit of God work in our midst, and that is unity." F. B. Meyer of the University of Liverpool made this intriguing observation: "The Swiss Family Robinson was always more interesting to me than Robinson Crusoe. The latter was alone on an island while the former was a family group. No man can be satisfied to live by himself. He needs fellowship with people!"

At the beginning of creation God made the statement: "It is not good that the man should be alone" (Gen. 2:18). Since the advent of time, each person has been created for fellowship with God and with other people. Emotionally, physically, and spiritually—it is not good for man to be alone. Medical doctor and novelist A. J. Cronin wrote, "Loneliness not only brings sorrow tomorrow—it saps today of its strength." A contemporary article on the talented Rod McKuen points out that the secret of his success has been his recognition of the deep and painful loneliness that pervades American society today.

Uprooted by two world wars, bewildered by a constantly shifting society that tends to dilute moral values, modern families are continually transferred from city to city and change houses almost as often as they do cars! One out of every five families in the United States will move this year, and they need to be a part of a New Testament Christian family called the church. Old family ties and social securities are changing. People have lost their identity in a rootless mobility, in the "anonymous living" of huge apartments and condominiums, in the isolation of suburbia! Is it any wonder that alcohol addiction is rising fastest among housewives trying to drown their loneliness in a bottle? Is it any surprise that the problem is compounded by baffled and bewildered people and the perpetually poor who are searching for a light out of the darkness, a love out of their gnawing, aching pains of loneliness?

In a world grown weary of superficial "togetherness," the church of Jesus Christ must dare to offer people a new kind of abiding union, a warm, winsome fellowship where people are loved in spite of their sins, unlovingness, and weakness, all because of the love of Jesus Christ.

On every hand today, in religious, legal, and political councils, the lonely cry from the lips of isolated people is for a united fellowship, but it is necessary to pause and ask a much deeper question: What kind of union will best adhere and grow strong?

Consider a fact from physics. When you moisten a handful of sand and press it together, it will seem to stick into a ball. But the moment the ball dries, the sand will crumble apart. On the other hand, if you gather a number of grains of iron dust around a common magnet, there will be a perpetual welding, and they will never fall apart.

The same principle applies to people. They may be forced together by some external pressure, but their union will be weak, temporary. When they embrace one common person and purpose, they become compacted into a cohesive whole.

Consider the amazing and creative unity in the Cave of Adullam. David's followers had come from all parts of Israel. Some were rough, and some were rich; some were ignorant, and some were learned; but as soon as they reached that cave, gathered around the magnetic personality of David, they were consolidated into a formidable fellowship. Against that united force, the whole kingdom of Saul was defeated and dispersed.

Remember the stirring story of King Arthur and the knights of the Round Table. What enabled this noble army to dispel the cloud of lawlessness throughout the whole country? It was the fact that King Arthur was in the center, the prince, in whom each unit found union.

The highest and deepest unity that can come to a New Testament church is the joining of hearts and minds and souls around Christ and his cause in the 1980s! It is not only the Polish people who yearn for solidarity; it is also the Christian people who need to be solidly united in Christ.

Listen to God's message in Philippians 2:1-2 "If there be therefore any consolation in Christ, if any comfort of love, if any fellowship of the Spirit, if any . . . mercies, Fulfill ye my joy, that you be like-minded, having the same love, being of one accord, of one mind." The duties of the Christian life cannot be borne in isolation. Its privileges cannot be enjoyed in solitude. The New Testament life requires fellowship with God in Christ Jesus and with other Christians. The word translated *church* in the New Testament means one thing only: a united fellowship.

This union is not static or nominal; it must be dynamic. Christ is the Creator, the cornerstone, and the King of his church. Members must develop a closer union with the divine Redeemer so that when they walk, they walk with Christ; when they talk, they talk with Christ; when they give, they give to Christ; and when they live, they live with Christ.

This Scripture points out three bonds of union for our fellowship in Christ; a comfort, a companion, and a cause. The first is called the comfort of "love." New Testament love has always been God's way to entwine the hearts of people. In the Christian fellowship, we discuss with each other, plan with each other, and pray with each other in the love of Christ. The new love program being initiated in many Baptist churches today encourages the members to thank, to encourage, and to ask forgiveness of the other members. This program tends to unite the church in Christ's kind of love.

Christ invites, "Come now, and let us reason together" (Isa. 1:18). If a member thinks every deed done in the church will be absolutely perfect, then he is hanging onto a twig that will snap and tumble into the dirt. The church is composed of people like the members today, and mistakes may occur. But we need to recall that no mistake needs to be malicious, none needs to be intentional. Underneath and surrounding every act must be the spirit of Christ's love. In the warm and gracious fellowship of the church of Jesus Christ, there is no place for malicious gossip, arrogance, or a judgmental attitude. Adlai Stevenson said, "He who slings mud always loses ground." If the members will be patient and understanding with each other, they can perform any service for Christ. Shared love puts a sparkle into todays' hours and a song into eternity.

It is not one of the main missions of the church to dispel the bad and the stale of the world and replace it with the good and pure of God? If one or two bees in a hive fan their wings, very little good would be done. But when they work in unison fanning together, they produce a breeze strong enough to snuff out a candle instantly!

Dr. H. A. Ironside told this story at a Bible Conference. A small Christian group which felt it was the only church was having a convention. Outside the auditorium they displayed a motto, "Jesus Only."

The first night there was a storm outside, and the wind blew away the first three letters. The amazing thing was that this particular group liked what was left so much that they did not change it during the convention; it read, "Us Only!" Needless to say, it was only a few years before this religious group had disbanded.

Anytime any congregation thinks it has arrived, that it's "Us Only," that it does not have to work together for Christ, then it has taken the road to death. As in the beehive, so in the church—every member has a job to do, and unless he does that job and cooperates with the other members the church will suffer, pale, and perhaps perish.

During World War II came a report from a secluded section of China, stating that a Japanese soldier entered a Christian Chinese church just before the service started. Fear and many misgivings showed in the faces of the Chinese Christians. They didn't know whether this soldier was a spy, an enemy, or a friend. Sensing their consternation, the Japanese soldier stood up and testified, "Brethren, I am a Japanese, but I am first of all a Christian. If you will permit it, I would like to worship with you." They welcomed him, and after the service he asked the pastor to sign his name in his Bible. The pastor added to his name, "In Christ there is no East or West, no Jew or Greek; all are brothers."

> Said a selfish old bee at the close of day,
> This colony business doesn't pay,
> I put my honey in that old hive
> That others may eat and live and thrive,
> And I do more in a day, you'll see,
> Than some of these others do in three!

> So the old bee flew to a meadow lane,
> And started a business all her own.
> She gave no thought to the buzzing clan,
> But was all intent on her selfish plan.

> But the summer waned and the days grew drear,

And the lone bee wailed as she dropped a tear,
For the animals gobbled up her little store,
And her wax played out and her heart grew sore.
So she winged her way to the old home band,
And took her meals at "the helping hand."

The second bond of unity is the living companion, the "fellowship of the Spirit." What a glowing assurance it is to know that a Christian never needs to enter an empty room or travel in solitude. We can tread the longest path without loneliness and speak for the living Savior in the power of his living Spirit. When we gather in the church as the soldiers of the cross, we stand united through the love of Christ and we commune with the all-powerful Spirit of the Living God!

In the New Testament church it is exciting to discover a comfort, the love of Christ; a companion, the living Spirit of Christ; and third, a dynamic cause, leading people to Christ. God's mercy has brought redemptive mercy to each one of us. Paul wrote, "I beseech you . . . by the mercies of God, that ye present your bodies a living sacrifice, . . . which is your reasonable service" (Rom. 12:1). It is not optional as to whether a Christian should witness or not. Every person who experiences the mercies of God is set apart as a sacrifice to serve and to lead people to Christ. He or she may be a candle or a thousand-watt bulb, but he or she is a witness.

Many have heard of Mel Trotter, the world-famed evangelist who led hundreds of people in Chicago to put their faith in Christ, but have you ever heard of how hard it was to win Mel Trotter to Christ?

Mel's second baby died because his father neglected him and was away from home in a drunken stupor. Trotter returned to the house for the funeral—not because his heart was softened, not because he was crying tears of repentance and remorse— Mel Trotter returned for his baby's funeral, so he could steal his own baby's shoes and sell them for more money to buy more booze.

And yet this same hardhearted Mel Trotter had a friend who prayed for him, told him about Jesus, persuaded him that Christ had the power to comfort, to keep, and to kindle a sacred flame of right living in any person's heart. Mel Trotter used to say, "I had the deafest ears, the hardest heart of any man in Chicago, but when my friend prayed for me and told me about Jesus' love on the Cross, it broke my heart and mended my life, and now I belong to Christ." Thanks be unto God for Christian witnesses!

J. Winston Pierce related this colorful story. The dean of women at Stetson University in Florida had reached the age of forty-nine and was still single. One day she was returning in the late afternoon to park her car, and she noticed that a student had parked his car in the space she normally occupied. It presented quite a problem because the dean of women had to park her car in that particular space. The man who brought the groceries for the cafeteria early the next morning had a key to her car, could move it, and then drive his truck up to the door to deliver the groceries. Of course, he would not be able to move another car.

The student was sitting in his car, and a pretty coed was with him. He had his arm around the girl's shoulder and they were staring out into space.

Well, you can imagine the anger, the chagrin, and the absolute disgust that passed over that pretty little coed's face when the dean of women drove up beside them, stuck her head out the window, and asked, "Pardon me, my dear, but can I change places with you?"

There is an adventure urgently needed today. No one can take your place in it, and that path is the strengthening of the fellowship of the New Testament church. An unnamed commentator has written, "The nineteenth century made the world into a neighborhood and the twentieth century must make the world into a brotherhood." On the one hand, we are trying to unite people by commerce. We bought the idea and advice, "Get the nations bartering and trading with one another, then the people will become better acquainted and will understand each other. The people will automatically make more money and make more friends." But this balloon has exploded in our faces today! Adam Smith, the colorful economist, has declared, "Commerce which ought to have been our greatest bond of world unity has become our most fertile source of discord and animosity."

On the other hand, we have tried to unite people with a higher form of culture and education. We have declared, "Lift the level of culture, increase the education of the people, and they will grow together." But these efforts have failed miserably. A leading educator has pointed out that our culture and education today are the most advanced in six thousand years, and yet our world is an armed camp.

Dr. Albert Schweitzer has observed that civilization at best is but a clearing in the midst of the jungle. At night, if you listen carefully, you can hear the growling of the wild beasts ready to pounce in and destroy civilization.

What united the early New Testament church into a fellowship, and what can unite a Baptist church today? The dynamic unity of the early New Testament church was not that the people looked alike, acted alike, or even thought alike in every case: it was that the people loved alike; they loved the Lord Jesus Christ; therefore, they could love one another. They had an uncommon allegiance to the uncommon Lord; therefore, they had a loving and uplifting allegiance to the Lord's church.

A husband and wife had been married for five years; they had fought, fussed, and fumed each day of those years. One day they had been screaming at each other for an hour when the wife suddenly stopped, marched over to the window, and poked out her mouth in a pout. The husband kept yelling for another five minutes before he ran down. Then, as he walked over to stand behind his wife, he glanced out the window and saw two horses pulling a heavily loaded wagon up the hill. The horses would slip back a bit, then they would pull together and make progress.

The husband said, "Love, look at those two horses working together and going forward together. Why can't we be like that?" Without changing her pout for a moment the wife replied, "Because one of us is a stubborn mule!"

Shifting the blame to someone else, being hypersensitive, wearing your feelings on your sleeve, being quick to criticize and slow to admit mistakes, choosing sides—not by what is right but by whom is right—by personalities rather than issues, taking the shortsighted rather than the farsighted view of Christ's plans for his church, saying in effect: "My mind is made up, don't confuse me with the facts!"—any of these attitudes are sand in the motor, square pegs in round holes, impediments to the progress and happiness and power of Christ's church.

Koinonia is the Greek word used repeatedly in the New Testament to describe the church as a fellowship. The Bible has no place for Christianity in isolation. No person can be as good a Christian on the golf course or on the mountaintop or at the seashore as he or she can be in the church. The Bible teaches that to be a good Christian one must be part of a good Christian fellowship, a good Christian family, a good Christian church! One clever wag has observed that when a banana leaves the bunch, it always gets skinned!

Christianity has never been a person-to-God relationship without also being a person-to-God-to-person relationship.

Even when monks withdrew from the world for contemplation, they withdrew in groups. They formed orders—fellowships of like-minded Christians—seeking together to be like Christ. Christians should be together in a Christian family to become the kind of Christians Christ intended.

Sometime ago, a sports reporter on NBC took his text and preached a rather powerful sermon in five minutes. He reminded his audience that one year Hank Bauer took a baseball team that everyone expected to end up in the cellar and won the World Series. Everyone in the baseball world was amazed, and at the usual banquet after such triumphs, they expected to hear some hot tips on how to take nothing and do something with it!

Bauer gave them surprising and realistic advice. "Friends, I guess we won about six games on brains and brilliant deductions, and we lost about six games on second guessing and stupidity. The secret is: if you can get twenty-five men pulling together, you can win any ball game!"

Christ calls the church a fellowship, and when Christian people gather together to explore the Word of God, to train in Christian maturity, to send out the good news of Jesus and his love, and to lift their minds and hearts to God in worship, it is the warmest and most winsome family fellowship on earth!

How can Christians be united in loving Christ, loving one another, and marching forward to make an impact for Christ upon this tottering old world?

Three suggestions come to us out of God's Word. One suggestion is that we make occasions to win friends for Christ. Charles Lamb walking along the street with a friend one day, burst out, "See that man across the street? I hate him!"

"Why, Charles, I didn't even know you knew that man."

"I don't know him. If I knew him I couldn't hate him!" responded Lamb.

Every seven and one-half seconds a new baby is being born in the United States, and the population grows by a new person every twelve seconds. The "sun belt" in which most of my denomination is concentrated is one of the fastest-growing areas of the nation. It is every Christian's task to make friends for the Master. When General Dozier was rescued in Italy, he kept on saying, "The prayers of the American people are what caused me to be reached and rescued." When people care, then others become their friends, and they can lead them to Christ.

Surely today we need to be reminded of the classic story of Jean Valjean by Victor Hugo. Here was a man who was released from prison after nineteen years, and no one would give him a job or food or lodging. Finally at the close of the day, he knocked on the door of a humble Christian. "Sir, my name is Jean Valjean. I have just been released from prison after nineteen years. No employer will give me a job; no restaurateur will give me any food; no landlord will give me any lodging. Can you help at all?" The Christian threw open the door of his home saying, "Come in, my friend. You didn't have to tell me who you were because this is Christ's house, not mine. You didn't have to tell me your name; I knew it even before you spoke: your name is brother!"

The old poet said, "To err is human, to forgive divine." It is natural that people will make mistakes from time to time, but when we know each other and discover why that person acts the way he does, then we can be more understanding and forgiving and gracious. For example, here's a man who lost everything he had in a financial fiasco. Now you might not approve his tightfisted, penny-pinching ways, but you can understand him better if you know his story. There is a lady whose husband has deserted her for another woman. This lady becomes exceedingly straitlaced and puritanical. At first she might be difficult to like, then when you knew her story you could understand her position. This does not imply that we are to go prying into other people's business, but this does mean that we have to be gracious, giving the other person the benefit of the doubt.

One of the charming stories told about Albert Einstein happened when he and Mrs. Einstein were returning from a trip to Europe. As they walked down the gangplank, they were immediately beseiged by reporters. One asked, "Mrs. Einstein, do you understand all about Professor Albert's theory of molecular construction?"

Mrs. Einstein smiled, "No, I do not understand all his theories, but I do understand Albert."

We are called to make occasions to make friends for Christ, and, second, we must look for the best in the other person. You will recall that the Greek word for cynic is the same word that they used for dog. The Greeks knew that if you look for the worst in the other person and become cynical, you will lead a dog's life. Some people's attitude is such that if another person does wrong they say, "Of course, what did you expect of him?" If another person does right, they say, "Wonder what he's getting out of this for himself!"

Jesus said, "Judge not, that you be not judged" (Matt. 7:1, RSV). Christ, our Lord, looked for the best and brought out the best in the other person. He did not put people down or criticize people. He challenged them to do the best that they could for Christ.

The story is told that an elderly man sat at an intersection of a road coming into his town, and a family drove up in a car with the children, the suitcases, the dog, and the goldfish, obviously on the move. The father asked the old man, "What kind of people do you have here in your town?"

The old man asked, "What kind of people did you find at the town from which you came?"

The husband exploded, "Oh, they were mean rascals. They were always trying to cheat us and take advantage of us!"

. The old man answered, "Well, you'd find those same kind of people here in this town; you'd better move on."

A half hour later, another family drove up, obviously on the move; and the husband asked, "Sir, what kind of people do you have here in your town?"

The old man asked, "What kind of people did you find in the town from which you came?"

"Oh," exclaimed the husband, "they were wonderful people! They welcomed us into the town, and they helped us feel at home among them!"

The old man extended his arm and said, "Drive right in here folks, you've found your new home, and we'll be glad to welcome you here!"

It is said that President and Mrs. McKinley were a deeply devoted couple. They were always looking for opportunities to show their love for each other. One day a horrible experience came as President McKinley was shot by an assassin. Even as he lay in intense pain knowing that the bullet would bring his death, the president whispered to a friend, "My wife is now sleeping. Don't wake her up too roughly. Break the news to her gently, very gentle," and he was gone. In Isaiah 41 we read, "They helped every one his neighbour; and every one said to his brother, Be of good courage. So the carpenter encouraged the goldsmith and he that smoothed with the hammer him that smote the anvil" (vv. 6-7).

Make occasions to make friends; look for the best in the other person as Christ looks for the best in you; the third suggestion is that we must be willing to lend a helping hand.

Fulton Oursler tells an inspiring adventure of an Indian Christian. Sadhu Sundah Singh was climbing a narrow mountain pass in Tibet with a Buddhist monk. It was in the dead of winter, and the path was covered with snow. They knew that they had to reach a nearby monastery by dark, or they would freeze to death. Suddenly, they heard a groan just over the ledge, and looking down they saw a man who had stumbled and fallen and was bleeding. The Buddhist monk said, "This is Karma or fate. It's his tough luck. He'll have to lie there and die, but I must look out for number one; I must press on to save my life."

Sadhu said, "My Christian faith teaches me to lend a helping hand." He climbed down the precipice, struggled to get the man up on his shoulders, and made his way back up to the path and pushed on. Finally, he came in sight of the lights of the monastery, but he stumbled and almost fell over something lying there in the snow. Looking down, he saw it was the same Buddhist monk who was looking out for number one and had frozen to death. By his very exertion of lending a helping hand, Sadhu not only saved his own life but the life of another person!

Isn't this the core of the Christian faith? The God of the whole universe saw us struggling and sinning, and he extended his hand to us in Christ Jesus; Christ extended his hand to us even from the cross, and we as his servants must be willing to extend a helping hand to those in need. Christ said that his church will be a warm and winsome fellowship if the members will make occasion to make friends for Christ, look for the best in the other person as Christ looks for the best in us, and be willing to extend a helping hand.

One of the deepest desires of all people is to grow up. Janis Joplin tried it without Christ but with drugs and literally blasted herself out of this world. Craig Baynham, former halfback with the Dallas Cowboys, is trying it with Christ through the Fellowship of Christian Athletes, and he is living literally on top of the world. In writing to the Philippians, the apostle Paul described a condition that is the dream of every true Christian.

Without pride but with the Spirit of the living God, Paul declared, "I have learned, in whatsoever state I am, therewith to be content. I know both how to be abased, and I know how to abound: ... I can do all things through Christ which strengtheneth me" (Phil. 4:11-13).

Wouldn't it be wonderful to be so mature in our Christian lives that in whatsoever state we found ourselves we could be content? Paul had lived a life of terror. He had walked through cities full of enemies; he had sailed through seas in the midst of severe storms. Paul had lived a life of persecution: he was cast into dungeons; he was lashed with a whip many times. Paul had lived a life of disputes: at Mars Hill, at Jerusalem, and all across the known world he had been a defender of the faith; yet in spite of peril, persecution, and disputes, Paul had learned to be content in Christ.

How did it happen? Paul uses the phrase in another letter that gives us a clue as to his contentment. He wrote in 1 Corinthians 3:1-9, "We are labourers together with God." Paul had the thrilling conviction that the God who called him out of darkness into his marvelous light, who created the universe and sent the planets revolving in their orbit, and who still cared and was continuing to recreate his world—this great God had some tasks for Christians to perform, and in their performance they would be working together with God! The exciting possibility was that Paul would be a partner with God!

It sent him to his knees for a prayer of thanksgiving. It lifted him up and thrust him out across the continent to picture for the world the life of the consecrated Christian. I heard Professor James Stewart say, "The rivers and hills around his home town, the lakes and mountains of Asia, became as nothing to this man, because beyond the hills and beyond the mountains there were men and women, boys and girls who desperately needed to know his Christ." The way for Christian people to be united in the 1980s is not to give gifts to each other, not to enforce external laws, but to be busy in a cause greater than themselves—to work and pray and witness in the greatest cause in all the world, the cause of leading people to Christ.

Where shall we begin? Right where we are with the people where we are. Children can be led to Christ in these days, and how important it is that the child be won to Christ early in life. Richard Baxter, one of the greatest pastors and preachers that England has ever seen, was converted at the age of six, not sixty! Jonathan Edwards, called the greatest thinker America has ever produced, was won to Christ at the age of seven. Isaac Watts, who wrote some of the greatest hymns in the English language such as "When I Survey the Wondrous Cross," was won to Jesus at the age of nine; and Henry Drummond, the brilliant Scottish chemist and preacher, was also won to Christ at the age of nine. Children can be won to Christ, and thereby they will receive their greatest blessing.

Adults can be led to Christ. Over and over again we find incidents where people thirty, forty, fifty, and older are being baptized. Those of us upon whom the light of Christ has shined are called to be partners with God in sharing that light. In sharing Christ, we can discover the greatest maturity and the deepest sense of purpose we have ever known. We can also capture the depth dimension of true unity in the Christian fellowship as we point others toward the One who is "the way, the truth, the life" (John 14:6).

4

The Church's Labor of Love Is Built on a Clue, a Climb, and a Closet
John 13:34 to 14:1

The genius of a strong church is that it believes the laity can make tremendous accomplishments for Christ. A layman had just become a Christian, and he volunteered for a job in his church. The pastor did not yet know his abilities but finally said, "OK, here is a list of ten men who are members of our church and who never attend, never give, and never participate. Here is some church stationery, and if you can't get an appointment with them you can send them a letter."

About a week later the pastor received a letter from one of the delinquent men, saying, "Dear Pastor, enclosed is a check for $1,500 to catch up on my offerings. Unless providentially hindered, I and my family will be back in Sunday School and church this Sunday. PS: Please tell your secretary that there is only one *r* in the word *dirty,* and no *c* in the word *skunk.*"

Laymen are the key to church progress, and the keynote of doing any job is adequate preparation. With those who have guided us in the past, we recognize that this is a day of rejoicing and praising God for the adventurous tasks that have been accomplished. People have been won to Jesus; other Christians have united with us in this labor of love! People have started studying their Bibles more! All members are growing in enthusiasm and are becoming more missionary minded! "Great is the Lord, and greatly to be praised" (Ps. 48:1).

As Southern Baptist churches face the mid-1980s, opportunities have exploded all around us! People need to hear the gospel!

People need to unite in the work of Christ! An inspiring statement was made by one of the most capable men in our church when he said to the nominating committee, "I'll take any job you ask me to try!" Indeed, every Baptist needs to be involved until every person is reached for Christ! The victories that are won tomorrow must be prepared for today.

We can prepare by asking this most important question: What does it take to make a real leader for Christ? What are the necessary qualifications? Certainly two necessities are a clue and a closet.

The students at the University of Edinburgh have an interesting expression. If you ask them a question, and they haven't the slightest inkling of an answer, they are likely to say, "I haven't the foggiest clue!"

You may recall Dr. B. F. Westcott of the University of London. His *Greek New Testament* is a standard text in many seminaries. One day a suffering student wrote to his friend: "A dense fog has just settled over London. This is largely attributed to the fact that Dr. Westcott has accidently left his study window open." There is enough foggy thinking abroad today, and the first necessity of a Christian leader is a clue—a personal knowledge of Christ. You cannot lead others if you do not understand where you're going. Someone said, "He who doesn't know and wants to learn is a student, teach him. He who claims that he knows but doesn't is a bluff, forget him. But he who knows and is capable of guiding is a leader: follow him."

Gibbon, whose *Rise and Fall of the Roman Empire* is a standard reference book in most colleges and universities, gave fifteen reasons why Christianity spread over the known world. He listed such things as a good organization, a clever message, a promise of life after death, a lot of enthusiasm; but with all his fifteen reasons, Gibbon missed the point entirely! The reason Christianity spread from person to person until it covered the entire Roman Empire was primarily because each witness knew Christ Jesus personally. No hearsay evidence convinced a person in that day any more than it convinces a person today. Listen to the blistering declaration in 1 John 1:1, "That which was from the beginning, which we have heard, which we have seen with our eyes, which we have looked upon, and our hands have handled, of the Word of life." No mental meandering, no vague theorizing here! "That which we" know from personal experience, that "declare we unto you" (v. 3).

The first letter of the apostle John gave us light. First John 5:13 reads, "These things have I written unto you that believe on the name of the Son of God; that ye may know that ye have eternal life." God has given this letter that our Christian lives might have security as well as sparkle, deep joy as well as dazzling jubilation, deep peace as well as high privilege. God does not mean for us to dawdle away in the doldrums of doubt: God means for the Christian's life to abound in blessings and beauty and benedictions. John was inspired to write that we can know for certain that we who believe in Jesus Christ have eternal life!

The question is, how? By faith and by actions. First of all, we must believe in this beautiful picture given to us by our Lord himself. In John 10:27 Jesus declared, "My sheep hear my voice, and I know them, and they follow me: And I give unto them eternal life; and they shall never perish, neither shall any man pluck them out of my hand. My Father, which gave them to me, is greater than all; and no man is able to pluck them out of my Father's hand."

Immediately someone says, "Oh, if I could only believe that, I would be the happiest person in town tonight! I'd have security and certainty in my heart. But look how many so-called Christians in this town will swindle and do anything they can to grasp other people's hard-earned money! See how many so-called Christians in this town will get so drunk on alcohol they have to be carried home like babies! Look how many so-called Christians in this town have their names on the church rolls, but they rob God by refusing to give their tithes, and they deny Jesus by refusing to let their influence count for Christ by serving in their church! No, I'd like to believe that a Christian is safe and secure, but the lives of so many so-called Christians make me wonder!"

The Word of God speaks just as plainly as this person. Listen again to the same letter: "They went out from us, but they were not of us!" (1 John 2:19). God's Word says that there are people who make a superficial profession of faith in Christ and display superficial allegiance to Christ's church, but they are just superficial. They are not true believers in Jesus Christ. Nowhere does the Word of God separate the belief a person professes from the life he practices. When Jesus says Christians are held in Christ's hand and God's hand and shall never perish because the omnipotent God has the power to keep them, Jesus means the real Christian, not some sham or pretender of Christianity.

This leads us to the second requirement for security and inspiration in your religion. First, you believe in Jesus' promise of eternal security, and, second, you must act on your faith to build love and harmony in your church. Read again this same searching letter: "This is the message that ye have heard from the beginning, that we should love one another. . . . we know that we have passed from death unto life, because we love the brethren" (1 John 3:11-14). As one commentator has observed, "You don't have to like every member of the church, but you do have to love every member with a love like the love of Jesus." Jesus' love always sought the best and highest for the other person. Jesus' love led him to work together with others to build God's kingdom into the lives of people.

In the last few years the First Baptist Church of Jacksonville,

Florida, has received a good deal of publicity. They are located right in the heart of a downtown business section, and they must have many new members every Sunday for their membership just to stay even! A few years ago they followed this practice. When the pastor gave the invitation for people to join the church, he would say, "Now brethren, we would be glad to welcome you into our fellowship, but if you have a record of gossiping, fussing, or breaking up the fellowship you came from, we would appreciate it if you would join some other church. We're trying to build a fellowship of Christian love here."

Over and over Christ himself said, "By this shall all men know that ye are my disciples, if ye have love one to another" (John 13:35).

If you have been living with a kind of uncertain religion, beset by darkness and doubt, and you really want a know-so religion, ask yourself these questions: Do I really believe Jesus' promise? Am I sure that the Christian is kept in the hands of God the Father and God the Son, and that no one can pluck them out? Second, am I doing all I can to build the love and fellowship of my church? Do I love the brethren, and does my life for Christ and the church reveal that love? Then, go on and ask the third question—the question that moves from your inner life to your church life and then out into the world: Does my daily life in the home, school, place of work reveal that I have been with Jesus? "Hereby we do know that we know him, if we keep his commandments. He that saith, I know him, and keepeth not his commandments, is a liar, and the truth is not in him. . . He that saith he abideth in him ought himself also so to walk, even as he walked" (1 John 2:3-6).

The Christian leader must have a clue, a personal experience of knowing Christ. Second, he or she must be willing to climb, to strive, and to grow in knowledge and commitment to Christ.

Third, he or she must also have the closet, the place of daily prayer where one can creatively commune with Christ and learn where Christ would have that person lead.

Robert Schumann composed some of the most beautiful music for the piano that has ever been written. But he died at an early age before he was able to give many concerts and acquaint the world with his music. His wife Claire bravely decided to play the concerts he had planned.

Each night, just before she walked out on stage to perform, she opened a locked drawer from her desk and read the letters she had received from Robert when they were growing in love. Then, with these love letters glowing in her heart she played such beautiful music that thrilling tears filled the eyes of her audience!

The Christian leader having read the love letters from Christ in the Scriptures must witness, win, and work with people until we all grow more like the Master. Dr. James Stewart declares, "The church today needs leaders who, knowing the world around them and the Christ above them and within, will set the trumpet of the gospel to their lips and proclaim Christ's sovereignty and all-sufficiency!"

Recently Billy Graham gave us a specific warning: "God is present on this planet; you didn't vote him in, and you can't vote him out!"

Dr. Adrian Rogers of the Bellevue Baptist Church in Memphis said to the Christian Women's Conference, "Build your homes and lives on the Word of God and reject the humanistic approach of attempting to solve the problems of mankind apart from God. Humanism is a way to hell: thinking they're too good to be damned, but they are in for a rude awakening!"

A modern scholar writes, "The difference between the early church and the church today is that the early church was power conscious, and the modern church is problem conscious." Like many of our clever sayings, this statement has an element of truth, but we need to probe a little deeper. We need to recognize that the early church had her problems, perhaps to the very point of seeing people as they really were rather than as they appeared. In Acts 6 and 7, we find a problem that could have really rocked the church, the problem of the distribution of the funds to the needy. But the disciples began the problem solving by prayer, faced each other in an atmosphere of trust, earnestly enlisted the leadership of God's Holy Spirit, and the problem was solved. How many heartaches and hurts could be healed today if we could prayerfully seek the fresh insight of God's Holy Spirit, search our own hearts, and serve with souls constrained by Christ's love! It is easy to give lip service to loving the whole world, but it is not always easy to love that individual person beside us for whom Christ died.

We need to begin with the tremendous inspiration of learning to love Christ, for it is as we learn to love Christ that we can learn to love one another. More than nineteen hundred years ago, twelve men with their Leader looked down from an upstairs window in an attic room with only a few candles burning. The darkness that slowly strolled down upon the earth did not remind them of a warm coat to bring them comfort: this darkness recalled the danger and the hatred that surrounded their very existence.

Some of the people walking in the streets below their window would gladly murder their Master. Some of these enemies believed they were heretics, others thought they were insane, and still others were convinced that they were trying to destroy the whole Jewish religion.

These twelve men needed to find the real source of strength. This need was determined, demanding, desperate. No pat on the back would meet their need. No futile illusion about brighter skies and better things tomorrow could answer their plight.

These men were caught in the clutches of danger: danger from the mobs and danger from their inner circle. It was as dangerous then as it is to be Jew or an Arab in the divided city of Jerusalem today.

In our day we have the same kind of need. Dangers from without are powerful, and dangers from within threaten our very existence. At this moment there is more insecurity in the hearts of our people than there has been in the history of our United States. Frankly, we are gripped by the gnawing power of fear. Like those twelve men nineteen hundred years ago we need a new lead to power, a new lease on power, and a new lean on power.

The world around baffles us; the people about battle us. We seem to get one problem solved, and suddenly five more break through! We live in a world of crisis after crisis. Our word *crisis* in the Chinese language has two characters: one means danger, and the other means opportunity. How can we discover the answer to our needs?

More than nineteen-hundred years ago the need was met. It was met in such a powerful way that twelve men transformed Christianity from a groping and despised religion to a global and dynamic religion. That need was met in such a powerful way that fishermen and farmers, lawyers and lumbermen, looked up from the routine and bordom of their everyday lives and caught a gleem of eternity! That need was met in such a powerful way that people who walked in darkness saw a great light, the light of God in Christ Jesus, and their lives were transformed by his love!

Perhaps you will say, "Well, that's great! I'm glad their need was met in such a powerful way. But I'm living nineteen-hundred years later. The question I want to ask is, how? How was their need met, and how can my need be met today? What can give me a new lead to God, a new lease on God, and a stronger lean on God?

In John 13 and 14 we have the scene portrayed. The twelve disciples were in tremendous need, and Jesus gave them a real way to solve their delimma: "A new commandment I give unto you, That ye love one another; . . . By this shall all men know that ye are my disciples, if ye have love one to another" (John 13:34-35).

What is the strongest motive to lead us to God? It isn't a duty or a demand or a dare; it is an honest love: love for Christ Jesus, the Son of God. It is not always by long lines of logic or by the torment of tragedy or by the thrash of thunder that men find God. The surest and deepest and most permanent way to be led to God is to love his Son, Christ Jesus.

In the same situation, Jesus explained, "If you love me, you will keep my commandments" (John 14:15, RSV). Every morning we need a new lease on God. If we love Christ, we will keep his commandments, and that will bring fresh experiences with God every day.

Too often, people become confused about the relationship between love and law. Some people think that Jesus should have said, "If you love me, you can do anything you please! If you love me you can break my laws anytime you please." But with piercing insight, Jesus explained, "If you love me, you will keep my commandments."

Some parents think they are loving their children by not making them keep their parents' laws. In truth they are ruining their children. Keeping the parents' rules enables the child to grow in love and respect for the care and wisdom of the parents. Mark Twain said, "When I was fifteen I was sure that my father was the most old-fashioned, ignorant, out-of-step man in our town, but when I became twenty, I was amazed at what the old man had learned in five years!"

We learn to love and trust God in the same way. The laws of God are perfectly fair and just. Christ fills full this perfect law; therefore, if you love Christ deeply enough you will keep his commandments and gain a new lease on God. Jane Lesson prayed,

> Saviour, teach me, day by day,
> Love's sweet lesson,—to obey;
> Sweeter lesson cannot be,
> Loving Him who first loved me.

A deep love for Christ gives us a new lead to God, a new lease on God, and it will also bring us to lean more on the everlasting arms of God! The greatest need of any church is not for new promotional ideas, new plans, new programs—the greatest need of any church is for Christian people, the church members, to humbly acknowledge their need of God and deepen their love for Christ! Yes, your church needs to be more active in Christ's service;—yes, your church needs to give more money for Christ's causes;—but your hands will never be truly busy for Christ until your heart beats with love for Christ. God wants and needs our work, God wants and needs our witness, but first of all and most important of all God wants us!

G. Campbell Morgan tells this meaningful story. A certain father and his daughter were great friends. Often they were walking together, laughing together, singing together. Then, suddenly, the father noticed a change in his daughter. When he went for a walk, she had to help mother. When it came time to go see the baseball game, she had lessons to do. It puzzled and grieved the father until one day he understood.

It was his birthday, and his daughter gave him a pair of wonderful slippers. "I made them myself, Dad, and I made them just for you." The father realized what had been happening the past several weeks, but he said, "Darling, thank you so much for these fine slippers, but next time buy the slippers, and let me have you with me every day. My daughter means more to me than anything she could ever give me."

My Christian friend, do you love Christ enough for Paul to say of you as he said of the Christians of Macedonia, "First they gave themselves to the Lord" and then their service (2 Cor. 8:5)?

Are you giving yourself in a growing, experiential commitment to Christ? Are you willing to climb toward Christlikeness? Are you continually sharing in the fellowship of the closed door for prayer? Certainly your church should be both the school of discipline and the powerhouse to generate prayer.

5

The Church Generates Prayer
Luke 11:1-9

The year 1850 was momentous in the life of Alfred, Lord Tennyson. In that year he married a girl whom he had been sparking for sixteen years but had been unable to marry because of "financial difficulties." Financial difficulties meant that he was so poor that even the poor people thought he was poor.

In that year he was named poet laureate of England, and he began one of his greatest works, *The Idylls of the King.* It was near the beginning of this great work that Tennyson made his famous plea, "Pray for me. More things are wrought by prayer than the world dreams of."

In Luke 11, we have the penetrating and inspiring question of Jesus's disciples, "Lord, teach us to pray" (v. 1). Some of the most profound New Testament scholars point out that these early disciples saw Jesus as he healed people, as he worked miracles in peoples' lives, and as he caused the natural phenomena to obey his will. But significantly, these disciples never asked Jesus to teach them to do any of these things. The only thing the disciples asked Jesus to teach them to do was to teach them to pray.

The early disciples watched Jesus as he went in to pray in one attitude and came out in another attitude. They watched Jesus pray for people, places, and events, and they saw lives changed because of Jesus' prayers! They witnessed whole atmospheres changed because of Jesus' prayers!

They therefore came to Jesus with the humble request,

"Lord, teach us to pray." Teach us to pray so that our lives, the lives of others, and the lives of whole nations will be drawn into the orbit of thy will!

Today we talk so much about power—nuclear power, air power, military power—but here is the greatest power in all the world, the power of prayer. A few weeks ago we went to visit a lady who is a shut-in. Her heart gives her a lot of trouble, and she isn't able to get out of the house very often, but she met us with one of the most beautiful smiles I have ever seen. Her whole face seemed to glow.

"Come in, Preacher," she said, "I'm mighty glad to see you." After we had visited for a while we had a prayer together, and this lady said, "Yes, sir, I surely do believe in the power of prayer. I had two boys in the service during the last war; one was in Italy, and one was in Germany. You know those boys said the reason they came back safely was because we all prayed for them, and they were right. God sure does answer prayer." Prayer can cause us to look up, realizing the tasks that must be done, the difficulties that must be faced, then to see beyond these present problems the hope-filled horizon and the help of Almighty God!

In James 4 we find these searching words, "Ye have not, because ye ask not. Ye ask, and receive not, because ye ask amiss, that ye may consume it upon your lusts" (vv. 2-3). Practical James makes two searching points: the first is that we do not pray enough today. "Ye have not, because ye ask not." The second point is an explanation of unanswered prayer, "Ye ask not, and receive not, because ye ask amiss."

Today, we talk a great deal about unanswered prayers. We say, "Why doesn't God intervene and make my loved one well? Why doesn't God bring peace in the Middle East? Why doesn't God solve my problems at work?" This sentence in the Scriptures reminds us of unoffered prayer. It suggests that we do not pray enough and blessings are denied us, not because they are unavailable but because we do not ask for them. We do not pray without ceasing.

Too often we neglect the closet with the closed door where Jesus says we are to pray to the Father in secret, and the Father will reward us. Christian men and women who go into the closet with the closed door come out with faces that shine and visions that shake the world. The apostle Paul began several of his letters with thanks unto God. Are we as thoughtful as we ought to be, and do we express our gratitude to God as often as we should? How different would be our daily lives if we prayed as we ought to pray!

Dr. George Truett told about a young man in Texas who committed a crime that broke his parents' hearts and will give them sorrow to their graves. A pastor of that community went to see the parents when he heard of their tragedy. As best he could, he counseled with them and comforted them. At last the sorrowing mother cried, "O sir, if I had prayed as I ought, this tragedy would not have happened."

The pastor begged her not to be too hard on herself for her sorrow was piercing enough without adding self-reproaches. But the mother continued, "I used to pray for that boy every morning, afternoon, and night, but that was in other years. In recent years my feet have been entangled in the pressures of meetings and time-consuming activities, and the things of Christ have had no practical place in my life. My priorities got mixed up; I have not been faithful to my church, and I have neglected to pray. Sir, this tragedy would not have happened if I had been faithful in prayer." As much as we sympathize with this lady, can we say that she is not speaking the truth? How different and more dynamic would be our lives if we prayed as we ought to pray!

What are some of the basic reasons for unasked and unanswered prayers today? The Bible raises four questions. First, is there a right attitude toward other people? Samuel Taylor Coleridge gave this insight, "He prayeth well who loveth well." The Bible wants to know if we have any malice, ill will, jealousy in our hearts toward other people. If so, we have an answer to our unanswered prayers. Jesus said, "When ye stand praying, forgive, if ye have ought against any: that your Father also which is in heaven may forgive you your trespasses" (Mark 11:25).

Again the Bible asks, "Is there a right life?" The psalmist explained, "If I regard iniquity in my heart, the Lord will not hear me" (67:18). One of the white-haired pastors at a meeting stood up to make this observation, "People today try to gloss over and smear over the wrongs in their lives and still yearn for peace in their hearts. We can never have peace without righteousness. Right living in the eyes of God is absolutely necessary before we can have peace of heart." The Bible says that it is the prayer of a *righteous* man, not an unrighteous man, that "availeth much" (Jas. 5:16). Again Jesus explained, "If ye abide in me, and my words abide in you, ye shall ask what ye will, and it shall be done unto you" (John 15:7).

A third question the Bible raises is this: Is there a right motive? If we casually conceive our prayers, certainly then we cannot expect them to be answered. Sometimes we stand with our hat in one hand, with one eye on the clock, and the other eye on the door ready to dash off someplace else. We need to be deeply sincere in our prayers, take time to commune with God, so that he will communicate with us.

Fourth, sometimes prayers go unanswered because of a lack of a right faith. Over and over we hear Jesus saying, "According to your faith, be it unto you" (Matt. 9:29). And again, "If two of you shall agree on earth as touching any thing that they shall ask, it shall be done for them of my Father which is in heaven" (Matt. 18:19). What an exciting promise! It challenges us to be

united in prayer! If we come together in the church to claim the
promise of God, he will make us a crusading army to attack the
strongholds of Satan, a spiritual hospital to heal and mend the
brokenhearted, a lighthouse to send forth the thrilling news of
Christ and his love and his power into the United States and
into the world! If two hundred or twenty or even two Christians
will pray earnestly, then lives will be transformed for Christ!

When the writer first moved to Mooresville, North Carolina,
several years ago, the telephone rang late one night and an upset
church member reported "One of our boys has just been rushed
to the hospital. They tell us he is critically ill."

When the pastor arrived, he learned that they had decided
not to take the boy out of the emergency room. The doctor was
shaking his head from side to side and saying, "This lad has
little chance to live."

The father was standing at the head of the bed, the mother
on the left side and the doctor on the right side. The mother and
father brushed away tears of worry and anxiety from their
faces. Then quietly and reverently, the mother, the father, the
doctor, and the pastor bowed their heads and lifted that boy to
God in prayer, praying that if it were God's will, the boy would
be healed. It was God's will. The boy's life was saved, and he
has now grown into a fine Christian young man!

What is so unusual or remarkable about this true story?
Absolutely nothing—when you remember that four people simply lifted their boy to God in prayer!

How it warms our hearts and strengthens our faith to realize
that our God can and does answer prayers whenever and wher-
ever he chooses! Betty Malz in her new book *Prayers That Are
Answered* shares with us this remarkable true story. She was
speaking at a luncheon meeting in Los Angeles and feeling that
the Lord had clearly led her to accept the invitation when a

person approached her secretively. "May I talk with you for few brief minutes—in private?" the inquirer asked.

A small conference room where several coatracks had been shoved aside to leave space for only two chairs was the only space available. She carefully closed the door and began her story. "Call me Ruth, but please don't ask me my full name for my husband's sake," she began. "I'm trying to keep his awful secret."

She looked out the window, checked the door again, and began, "My husband is a professor at a state college not far from here. He left me for another woman. My heart's breaking just like our broken home. I can't even cry any more."

After she struggled for composure, she continued. "You said today, 'If you can trust, all things are possible.' Do you think prayer and trust would change not just a circumstance, but a mind . . . my husband's mind?"

Betty replied, "Yes, I do. The Bible tells how Jacob wrestled with an angel and his nature was changed." Looking at Ruth, she found it hard to believe that a husband could desert her. She had a pleasant voice, an air of quiet elegance like Princess Grace of Monaco. The few silver-gray strands that streaked her dark hair were highlighted by her silver earrings and neck chain which perfectly matched her dark plum, suede dress.

"For several months now my husband has been living in an apartment with his young secretary." she continued. "I have kept his secret, thinking he would soon come to his senses and realize that this girl is the same age as our married daughter, that he would see how foolish this fling really was. I do not want his students to know. They would lose confidence in him."

The lady was clasping her hands together and twisting them nervously as she continued: "One morning this past week I was sitting alone in our breakfast room drinking a cup of coffee watching the birds having their breakfast on the bird feeder.

Suddenly my husband drove into the driveway. I was so glad that I had brushed my hair and put on the breakfast coat that he had so much liked. It has lilacs printed on it. When he was getting out of the car, I poured him a cup of coffee and placed it on the table next to mine. I tried to be cheerful when I let him in the side door.

"He merely stepped inside and shook his head when I asked if he wanted a cup of coffee. He just stood there, rigidly, and said, 'I'm glad you're up and awake. I was on my way to the school for my first class and decided to stop instead of calling you on the phone. Debi is not satisfied with our arrangement. She wants a husband and children. Please file for a divorce on the grounds of adultery. It will make it easier for everyone.' When he left, I was so discouraged and upset that I wanted to die."

Betty squeezed the lady's hand and assured her that they would pray right then. "Heavenly Father, you are the Healer of bodies and the Restorer of broken relationships. Please repair this marriage, restore it, and replace this woman's sadness with joy. Make a bridge of Ruth's broken dreams, and form a rainbow of all her tears. Clear up the confusion in the mind of her husband. Touch his heart, lead him to repentance. We pray this for Debi, too, that she see that the way to a home with children is not through stealing another woman's husband. Cleanse this whole situation, Lord, in the name of Jesus."

The date of this speech was December 9. Ten days later on December 19, Betty was in Houston, Texas, speaking to a Christian women's club luncheon. The subject was Christmas prayers, and toward the close she reminded the ladies that for Christmas God would restore broken hearts, broken homes, and give us the desires of our hearts if we would ask him in prayer. When things are right between us and others, we will have his presence to make Christmas more meaningful than the presents. Then Mrs. Malz prayed, "Lord Jesus, we feel your power beginning to answer our prayers right now. If there is anyone here who has never received you, who needs your forgiveness, who yearns for the life eternal you promised, nudge them now, Lord. Touch their hearts. Move them to a decision."

At that point Betty happened to open her eyes to see a shapely young woman in a pink jersey dress walking out the door. She thought the young woman was ill.

After the prayer, several people remained behind discussing the message. Betty saw the young woman return, place her head down on her arms for a few minutes, then sit up.

As Mrs. Malz was leaving the banquet hall, she stopped and was talking to one of the waitresses when this same young woman who had walked out during the prayer came up to her. She waited until she had her full attention, then suddenly threw her arms around Betty's neck and began to weep uncontrollably. She apologized for getting the front of Betty's dress wet with her tears, then she told her story.

"I am home for the Christmas holiday visiting my parents. I had not planned to come to this luncheon. When I saw your picture in the paper, I remembered your book in a book store window at the college where I work in California. On a strange impulse I decided to come and hear you talk. I thought you would talk about your book."

She found it hard to go on, and Betty, with an inner knowing, put her arm around her. The girl continued, "When you said that God would restore broken homes if we asked in prayer, I could not sit there any longer. I went out to the lobby and called long-distance to my boss in California. I have been working as a secretary to a college professor. We became very close, and he moved in with me, promising to marry me.

"I guess I was selfish because I did not think about his wife until I was convicted by what you said. Well, I told him I was resigning as his secretary. I told him to go home to his wife and beg her forgiveness, then to ask God to forgive him, because that was exactly what I was going to do. I am going to stay here in Houston with my parents and get myself straightened out. I feel clean inside now. Thank you for waking me up. Thank you for teaching me about prayer."

Four days later Betty received this remarkable letter:

DEAR BETTY,

God has answered prayer in mysterious ways since you were here. Debi phoned a few days ago and turned my husband down, just plain dropped him and quit her job. Last night my husband came, and we talked about it for the first time.

Before going to bed, we knelt together to pray with our arms around each other. God forgave him there, and I had forgiven him several days ago.

In bed, while lying on his arm, he caressed my face and told me, "I almost came back on December 9. But after ruining Debi's reputation I didn't have the nerve to tell her I had changed my mind. I was also afraid that you would not have me back." I asked him what caused him to change his mind. "I can't explain it. It was like I had been arrested by an unseen policeman and told, 'Go home!' he said.

You're right. Nothing is impossible with prayer.

Thankfully,

RUTH[2]

What would be a good job description for the prayerful leaders of the church?

6

The Church Presents a Job Description for Her Leaders
Exodus 3

According to the latest statistics just released from Washington, we are adding 8,000 people to our planet every twenty-four hours! In the next four decades, we will have global wars and global massacres unless we have a spiritual awakening! We must listen to God's Word to Moses in Deuteronomy 2:3, "You have been going about this mountain country long enough; turn northward and command the people" (RSV). We must be spiritually aware, spiritually alert, and spiritually alive to God's leadership if we are going to meet God's challenges for these days.

In Exodus 3 we discover one of the most dramatic calls to leadership in all the Scriptures. God looked upon his people with all their needs for repentance, refreshment, revival, and God called a leader to help meet this people's needs.

Moses was tending his father-in-law's flocks in the land of Midian. He was passing over ground that had become familiar and beloved to him when suddenly he saw an arresting sight! Moses heard a crackling noise like cellophane on fire, and his eyes fell upon a blazing bush! He knew not how the fire was started, but the surprising thing was that the flames were leaping all around the trunk, and the green leaves were not turning yellow and charred; they stayed green as they blazed with fire! Such a strange and curious sight would capture anyone's attention!

But the burning bush was not all. With no apparent microphone or telephone connection, a voice came out of the blaze calling, "Moses, Moses!"

"Here I am, Lord."

"Do not come any closer. Take off your shoes because this place is holy ground. I am the God of Abraham, of Isaac, and of Jacob." Moses hid his face and slipped to his knees in worship.

God said, "I have seen the acute need of my people, and I have come to deliver them. Through you I will lead the children of Israel into the Promised Land, the land flowing with milk and honey."

Moses asked, "But when I come to the Israelites and they say, 'Who sent you?' whom shall I answer?"

God replied, "I AM THAT I AM. Say unto the children of Israel, 'The God, I AM, has sent me.' Let all our people serve our eternal God."

In this divine-human encounter, we see all the necessary prerequisites of a Christian leader. Moses was in the right place, he took the right position, and he held to the right purpose.

Each year each church finds it necessary to take an inventory to examine their goals and to explore their leadership. The church is grateful for the personal devotion to Christ and the personal dedication to Christ's cause of each leader. The leaders have brought forth the fruits of love, justice, unity, and faith in the lives of the members. What does God's Word say about the leaders' requirements for the future?

First, they must be in the right place. When Moses heard God's call, God said, "The place whereon thou standest is holy ground" (v. 5). There can be no substitute for a Christian leader's regular attendance in the holy place, the church. The leader is not supposed to hold a major office in every phase of the church's ministry, but he or she is called to be loyal and regular in attendance in Sunday School, Church Training, the worship services, and the prayer meetings. God calls every Christian leader to experience the worship of God in the right place, the holy place, the church.

Suppose you asked a friend, "What is a rainbow?" He might take you to the edge of a river and stick in a cane pole. You would see that the pole seemed to bend in the river, and he could explain to you the principle of light refraction. Alternatively, your friend might write out a complicated equation of physics and explain it to you that way. But who would say that a pole in a river or an intricate equation from a physics lab was really a rainbow? Could either of these capture the magic, the marvel, the sheer glory of God's vivid promise in the heavens? Of course not, nothing can take the place of a real, radiant rainbow.

In these days of counterfeit coins and counterfeit consciences, our deepest desire is for a real religion. Absolutely nothing can take the place of a firsthand knowledge of Jesus Christ. The cry from every person today is, "Away with your filmy speculations; away with your futile fancies, we want the facts! Away with your theological enigmas and moral rationalizations, we want reality!"

In Acts 19 we see a vivid illustration of the futility and fatality of a secondhand religion. By the Spirit of God, Paul had been able to cast out demons and restore people to their rightful minds. Sceva, the chief priest, had seven sons, and they all seethed with envy toward Paul. They reasoned among themselves, "Paul uses a magic formula, 'by Jesus,' and miracles seem to happen. Why can't we try the same thing?" Before a huge crowd, these seven sons dragged a man with an evil spirit. "We command you by Jesus whom Paul preaches to come out of this man!" There's your secondhand religion. They knew Paul's Jesus, not their own Jesus.

You can imagine the result. The evil spirit cried, "Jesus I

know, and Paul I know; but who are you?" (v. 15, RSV). The man who had the evil spirit leaped on these jealous sons and whipped the fire out of them. They had to dash for home with blood streaming from their noses, and their torn clothing flapping in the breeze! Two facts are clear about a secondhand religion. In the dangerous day it is insecure, and in the dreary day it is ineffectual. C. E. Montague of the University of London points out that all the best part of experience lies in the discovery that ordinary pieces of observation are shiningly and exhilaratingly true.

We Christian leaders need to think of the proven phrases of the religion that we may have spoken this past year as if they were platitudes, bleak to us and boring to our hearers. Sometimes we may have declared the love of God, the loveliness of the Holy Spirit, and the longing of Christ without a ghost of a thrill as if it were a drab and dry gospel.

Think of Thomas Chalmers in the manse at Kilmany, Scotland. For years he was quite content to teach a cold, formal religion. But one day, he had a personal encounter with God in Christ Jesus. From that moment on, he preached to save. "Mathematician as I was," he said, "I had forgotten two magnitudes—the shortness of time and the vastness of eternity." Then Christ transformed his life, and his drab, dreary gospel came alive; now it had hands, and feet, and a heart throbbing like the heart of God.

"I had heard of thee with the hearing of the ear," confessed Job to God, "but now mine eye sees thee" (Job 42:5, RSV). The old psalmist burst into the sunlight of a personal encounter with God and sang, "O God, Thou art my Lord" (Ps. 16:1-2).

When the church nominating committee considers a person for a specific task, what do you think should be the first requirement? Actually, they should not begin by asking what special aptitudes this person possesses. They should start with this question: Does he or she know Christ personally, and has he or she professed that knowledge by uniting with the church and living for Christ daily?

We can have this personal encounter with God and Christ by longing and listening.

Picture a small group of Samaritan peasants huddled under a blazing sun. News has reached them that the promised Messiah is passing through their land. How their hearts beat faster at this exciting but incredible news! How they yearn to throw off their yoke of heartache and sadness and sin! How they long to know this Christ! Suddenly their steaming daydreams are shattered by a cry. "Come," said the woman, "see a man who told me all that I ever did. Can this be the Christ?" (John 4:29, RSV).

Half doubting but still longing they went out to Jacob's well, and they came face-to-face with the Christ. Returning, they wore a smile of complete peace. "It is no longer because of your words that we believe, for we have heard for ourselves, and we know that this is indeed the Savior of the world" (v. 42, RSV).

We have personal experiences with Christ by longing to have them and by listening to God in the daily practice of prayer. God will never reveal himself to the person who never prays. Pray when you feel great. Pray when you're tired. Pray when you win the prize; pray when you lose. Pray until your prayer line becomes electric and alive with God's commands, God's comforts, and God's concerns.

Christian leaders need to be in the right places, and second they need to assume the right attitude. I feel that the moment Moses heard the voice of God, he closed his eyes and bowed his knees in reverence and prayer.

When another pastor was visiting in our church, we invited him to join the deacons' prayer meeting before the worship service. "Do the deacons always meet for prayer before you go to worship?" he asked.

"Yes, sir."

"Then," said he, "I can see where this church gets her power!"

There is no substitute for Christian leaders with reverence and personal prayer in their lives. It must be repeated over and over again until it is practiced. We shall be mere whirling weather vanes, and we shall vainly try to fan into a flame the cold ashes of a dead congregation until every Christian leader in the church goes to God daily in prayer! Prayer puts us in touch with the God who made us, the God who made the church, the God who can constantly remake us after his own likeness. Before the church can ever be a people of divine power, the members must be a people with dedicated prayer lives!

The right place, the right position, and each Christian leader must have the right purpose. God called to Moses, "My friend, our people are in deep need. This need is like a sword, sticking into my heart and stirring my brain. Wouldn't you like to help me meet the people's needs?"

Moses was happier than he had ever been in his life in Midian: wife, children, flocks, friends, everything was in Midian. It would mean tremendous danger and sacrifice to return to Egypt. But something happened to Moses in that divine-human encounter. As he heard God's call to service his eyes were opened, his heart was stirred, his mind was inspired. Moses began to see people in need, at least in part like God sees people in need. The opportunity of laboring together with God set a high purpose blazing in his heart; at all costs, in spite of danger and sacrifice, he must help God love the people and revive the people.

God is calling today, not through a burning bush on a Midianite hillside but through the inner voice of his Spirit in each Christian soul—be in the right place, the church; take the right position, the position of reverence and prayer; and hold unswervingly to the right purpose, laboring together with God to meet people's personal needs.

A keen raconteur shares a dream with us:

The other afternoon I was reading the newspaper when I suddenly heard a terrific crash just outside my window. I rushed out into the dusk dark and came upon a man bending over and picking up pieces of broken plastic. It seemed to have been one of those plastic models of a church, but now it was smashed to bits.

"Hey, man, what are you doing?"

As he straightened up and turned toward me, I could see the nail prints in his hand and the thorn prints in his forehead; and again, but more reverently, I asked, "Lord, what are you doing?"

The Master answered with a magnetic smile, "I'm putting this church together to serve people, wouldn't you like to help?"

When the leader is in the right place, taking the right position, holding unswervingly to the right purpose, he will want to guide the church in the practical and spiritual matter of Christian stewardship.

7

Grumblers and Grudgers Are Transformed into Gracious Givers

Genesis 28:16-22

At the Savannah River Baptist Association, John Roberts of the *Baptist Courier* quoted this paraphrase:

Mary had a little lamb,
It would've become a sheep,
It became a Southern Baptist
And died from lack of sleep!

B. F. Skinner of Harvard declared, "American civilization today is running away like a frightened horse! Its speed and panic increase together while politicians and others wave their arms wildly in despair of giving direction." There is a God-created organism that is called not to be conformed to the world but to transform the world, and the church of Jesus Christ can do it if each member plans, participates, and pursues Christ's opportunities! *Changing Times* magazine states, "Today there's one sure way to save on your food budget—plan your meals wisely, buy in bulk, and eat your Thanksgiving dinner over at Mom's house!"

John Maynard Keynes, who is quoted so often as an economist, wrote, "I see us free to return to one of the sure principals of religion—that greed is a vice, that the exaction of usury is a misdemeanor, and that the love of money is detestable. . . . We shall once more value ends above means and prefer the good to the useful if every citizen will participate in what is good for the country."

There are at least two types of church members who miss the deeper meaning of giving their tithe to Christ through the church. The first type is composed of the grumblers. It's true in the church as it is true in business, in the home, and everywhere else—the people who grumble and gripe the most are usually the people who "put out" the least. When people are really working and serving the Lord, then they do not have the time or the interest to growl and grumble. An old Indian adage reads, "He who is pulling the oars has no time to rock the boat."

A certain family returned home from church one Sunday, and almost every member had a few thousand unkind words to say: the father was turned off by his Sunday School lesson; the mother thought the sanctuary was too hot and stuffy; and the daughter exclaimed, "That music was just for the birds!" But they all became strangely quiet when little Jimmy popped up with, "Well, anyway, Dad, don't you think it was a pretty good show for the quarter you dropped in the offering plate?"

There are also some people who fall into the category of the grudgers. They give regularly to Christ through his church, but they give grudgingly, out of a sense of duty rather than out of a heart of love.

In Edinburgh, Scotland, they have a small candy store called a Sweety Shop in almost every neighborhood. One afternoon I stopped in our local Sweety Shop and came upon a mother holding her little daughter in her arms. Apparently, she had just bought the child a bag of candy, and the child was clutching it as if it were pure gold. Since I was a total stranger, I simply smiled at the little girl and started to move on, but I could tell that she was having a tremendous struggle in her mind.

She looked at me, then she opened the bag of candy. She frowned in concentration as she seemed to be counting each piece in the bag. Then she turned her head away, scowled, and thrust the bag of candy under my nose. There could be no doubt about the enormity of the sacrifice she thought she was making. Probably her parents had taught her to be thoughtful to strangers, and she felt that she just had to offer a piece of her candy.

Isn't this a vivid picture of the way some people give to the Lord? The reason, "I know God's Word commands me to tithe, I know Christ commended the tithe, I know my church could use the tithe, so I guess I'll be forced to give the tithe."

What is really the best reason to give at least a tenth of your total income to Christ through his church? Should you do it to promote a large program? No. Should you tithe to win the personal recognition of your friends and increase your personal prestige? No. What, then, is the best reason for giving God one tenth of your total income through your church?

There is a striking analogy in your windowpanes at home. Go and look out of the front windows of your home: What do you see? You'll see men and women, boys and girls, passing by with their various needs. Now, having seen the people, go over and look at your largest mirror: What do you see? You will see yourself. Consider it a moment. What is the basic difference between the glass in your mirror and the glass in your window? The difference is that the glass in your mirror has been silvered. It is the silver that stands between you and the other people with their needs.

Immediately, we see the application: the more you give away the silver, the less you see of yourself and the more you can see of the other people and their needs. What is the strongest reason for giving the tithe and more to Christ through his church?

The most penetrating, persuasive, personal reason is that Christ loves people and gave himself to meet their needs! Because we are Christians, because Christ has called us into the orbit of his love that we might share that love, we gladly give our tithe to Christ through his church to help meet people's needs.

God's Word says, "God loveth a cheerful giver" (2 Cor. 9:7). The greek word here is *hilarons* from which we get our English word *hilarious.* God loves the person who gives happily, cheerfully, hilariously! What makes the giver so cheerful? The wonderful feeling of knowing deep in his or her heart that by giving money he or she is sharing the love of Christ with people in need. Consider how many more missionaries could be sent, how many more young people could receive a Christian education, how many more homeless little children could be provided for, how many more elderly people could have their sunset years transformed if every member of your church would be loyal to Christ and loved Christ enough to pledge and give a tithe!

Brooks Hays, former president of the Southern Baptist Convention, died recently. He was elected and served many terms in the United States Congress, but one time he ran and was defeated. A friend was sympathizing with him when Brooks answered simply, "Thank you for your concern, but I follow the One who taught that by giving we get and by dying we give!"

Bishop Earl Hunt of the Western Conference of the Methodist Church in North Carolina is quoted in the newspapers as saying, "If we want to see a revival among our people, renewal among our churches, it will come only as Methodists tithe their time and money!" Carl Bates, former president of the Southern Baptist Convention, gives this insight: "It was in the year 1963 that we had the slogan and made the effort—'Every Baptist a Tither!' It was in that same year that we won more people to Christ than we have ever won before!"

As Baptists we have always sought to be the people of a Book and that Book the Bible! We place the pulpit in the center of our churches because the pulpit holds the Word of God, and God's Word is our rule of faith and practice.

How much of God's Word is concerned about the spiritual use of money? Did you realize that the New Testament speaks more about giving than about any other subject except how to be saved? Jesus told thirty-eight parables, and sixteen of them concerned material possessions. One out of every six verses in the Gospels of Matthew, Mark, and Luke discusses the spiritual use of money. The Bible as a whole mentions prayer a little more than 500 times, faith a little less than 500 times, but the Bible as a whole speaks of the spiritual use of material possessions over 1,000 times! If the spiritual use of money is so important to God's work, then surely it is of paramount importance to God's people! If you give at least 10 percent of your total income first (and more to Christ through his church), save the second 10 percent, and live within the remaining 75-80 percent, then you will really live.

How does God's Word say we are to give? In Genesis 28:22, Jacob with keen inspiration dedicates himself to God: "And this stone, which I have set for a pillar, shall be God's house: and of all that thou shalt give me I will surely give the tenth unto thee." Consider God's invitation to pilgrimage in Malachi 3:10: "Bring ye all the tithes into the storehouse, . . . prove me now herewith, saith the Lord of hosts, if I will not open you the windows of heaven, and pour you out a blessing, that there shall not be room enough to receive it." In Matthew 23:23 Jesus Himself added, "These ought ye to have done." Tithing is reasonable, rewarding, and always reverent.

First of all, tithing is an intelligent, reasonable service to God. What are some of the objections people raise today to tithing? One person expressed it this way: "It's *my* money. I worked hard and earned it, and it's mine!" Did anyone at any time or any place earn anything without the help of God? Of course not! Who gives us the will to work, the health to work, the strength to work? Surely it is God. Over and over God's

Word reminds us that we are not our own, we were bought with a price. All we have, and all we can accomplish are gifts from God; you couldn't possibly earn a penny without God. Isn't it reasonable to give him his part?

Another objection is expressed in this way, "Right now I'm in debt, and I can't afford to tithe." Most people are in debt today for various reasons. But God's Word does not say, "All of you who are not in debt, bring your tithes into the church." God's Word says to every Christian, "Bring ye all the tithes into the storehouse." When we consider it honestly, to whom are we most in debt? To the gifted salesperson, to the grocer, or to the garage worker, or to God? Romans 8:32 says that God has freely given us "all things," and in James 1:17, "Every good gift and every perfect gift is from above, and cometh down from the Father."

A third objection raised is this, "It costs too much! Ten percent is too high!"

A pastor in Atlanta won a Communist to Christ, and they began talking about Christian obligations and opportunities. The former Communist asked, "How much time am I to give to Christ?" The pastor answered, "Well, we are to attend Sunday School, Church Training, prayer meeting, worship services ..."

"That's amazing! When I was a Communist I gave three hours a day seven days a week to the cause of Communism! How much money am I to give to Christ?"

"The Bible says at least 10 percent of our income."

"That's astounding! When I was a Communist I gave 50 percent, half my salary! Christ's obligations and opportunities are most reasonable."

Tithing is not only a reasonable service: it is also a rewarding service to God. We do not give primarily to receive a reward, but we would paint an incomplete picture without including the latter part of Malachi 3:10, "Prove me now herewith, saith the Lord of hosts, if I will not open you the windows of heaven, and pour you out a blessing, that there shall not be room enough to receive it."

A certain farmer in Sumter, South Carolina, felt God's call to preach the gospel. He had a wife and three children and no other treasures. For years he had tithed his income, and he reasoned, "The Lord has not made us rich, but he has certainly cared for us in a wonderful way." With seventy-five dollars, he and his family left for the Southern Baptist Theological Seminary in Louisville, Kentucky. He tried to get a job outside school hours, but he couldn't. His meager funds soon ran out.

On Friday he had only fifty cents and very few groceries. What could he do? He prayed for God's guidance, and in the last mail on Saturday he received a check for fifty dollars from his home church. Fifty dollars would not go very far with five people to feed. He had no assurance of getting more money the next week. He and his wife went to their knees and prayed earnestly to know God's will. The next morning they gladly put a tithe in the offering plate of the church, and God so blessed them that they were able to stay on for six years at the seminary, and the husband was able to earn a doctor's degree. Yes, tithing is a reasonable and rewarding way to grow in spiritual maturity. Joe Gandolfo of Lakeland, Florida, sells more life insurance than any other agent in America. Joe testifies that he has given more than a tenth through the years, and each of his clients who is a really big hitter—really successful—gives more than a tenth to God.

Third, tithing is most important of all a reverent service to God. The giving of the tenth has no higher motive and no deeper meaning than to strengthen our love relationship with the living God. One scholar wrote, "Your heart and your pocketbook are Siamese twins." Christ in the Sermon on the Mount puts it this way, "Where your treasure is, there will your heart be also" (Matt. 6:21).

Each of us gives or fails to give God his part precisely on the basis of our love relationship. If we are found faithful and give God his part, it is because of our love.

In a financial journal this statement was made: "Since the first coin came from the first mint, men have been divided into two groups—those who work for money and those who put money to work for them." Dr. Halford Luccock claims, "They have missed the most important group—those Christians who love the Lord enough to give their tithe and more to Christ through this church and put money to work for God!"

Jimmy's father died when he was only ten, and his mother went to work to support their large family. As soon as he was able, Jimmy got a paper route. He gave his mother most of the money, but he saved some of it to buy her a birthday present.

He decided on roses, and he explained to the florist, "These are for my mother's birthday, so please give me the prettiest roses you have." For perhaps the first time in florist history, 89 cents bought a dozen, beautiful red roses.

Jimmy was thrilled; but as he started across the street, there was a screech of brakes, a gentle thud; Jimmy and the roses were scattered across the pavement. When Jimmy waked up in the hospital, the first thing he saw was his battered bunch of roses. The little boy whispered, "Take these to my mother. They were the best I could find, and tell her that I love her."

Yes, after all the logic and the learning, the lists have been stacked to the ceiling; you give or fail to give God the tenth on the basis of your love. It is love that makes the signing of your envelope and the presenting of your tithe an act of worship. Tithing is a reasonable, rewarding, and, most important of all, reverent service to God.

If you are already tithing, you know the deep joys of God's

bountiful blessings. If you have not started tithing, try this Christian adventure for three months, and you will discover how great it is to be right with God!

When a person gets right with God in the area of Christian stewardship, there are always new depths to be fathomed, new insights to be gained, new horizons to be conquered, and new inspirations to be given as he or she goes forward for Christ.

8

Discouragers and Disparagers into Expediters and Encouragers
Hebrews 13:11-13

John A. Broadus was chairman of the department of preaching and president of the Southern Baptist Theological Seminary back in the days when it was fashionable among Baptists and other Christians to downgrade and distrust education. One day Dr. Broadus was visiting in an association out from Louisville when one of the brethren thought he would cut down the president of the seminary by praying very fervently, "O Lord, please make me ignorant, make me ignoranter than a mule!"

Dr. Broadus whispered to a friend nearby, "You have just seen the Lord perform a miracle. The Lord answered that prayer even before it was asked!"

On television a comedian defined middle age as the time when the broad mind and the narrow waist change places! The tragedy is that this condition affects people of all ages in the mid-1980s. Today we live in the most unconsidered and unbridled, divided and disagreeing world in history. One football coach reports that another coach is out recruiting football players who are "agile, mobile, and hostile."

When you visit a young couple who has just moved to your city, you will often find that they are hungry to discover in this frayed and frightened world a fellowship of people who are genuinely united. The word that Jesus used most often to describe the divinely conceived and divinely created body called the church was the Greek word *koinonia*. This word has just one meaning: a Christian fellowship. Christ was and is willing to risk the outcome of his magnificent kingdom to the group of Christians called his church, precisely because Christ loved the church: Christ gave his life for the church, and Christ longed for the members of his church to first love him, then love one another with this dynamic, Christian kind of love.

This means, first of all, that it is an actual sin for any member of the church to speak disparagingly and to cause a division within the Christian family of the church. Sometimes people speak too hastily before they have the facts, then after the injury has been done it is too late to call back that hasty word or that discouraging remark. Christ teaches us that every Christian should guard his tongue and his thoughts carefully. Jesus asked such pointed questions as: "Why do you consider the splinter in your brother's eye and forget about the two by four in your own eye? Why are you so quick to judge another?" It is better to compare your life to the life of Christ, exercise judgment upon yourself, and seek to correct your own faults than to be so quick to criticize or judge another person.

Here in our church when a couple comes for counseling before their marriage, the pastor discusses with them the basic principles of a Christian marriage. One of the principles is mutuality. In this discussion the pastor says something like this: "You have probably heard couples say that they have been married for fifty years and have never had a cross word. That would be rather dull even if it were true which is doubtful. In a Christian marriage you must remember that you do not bring a perfect person to the marriage; therefore, you can afford to be gracious and slow to anger, slow to criticize the other partner in your marriage."

This same principle applies in the Christian family of the church. Christ intends the members of the church to be a gracious, Christ-like fellowship, and the members must control their impulses to anger, to comparison, to criticism! The members are called to strengthen the Christian fellowship, never to weaken it.

This means not only negatively that the members are not to exercise hasty judgment and be quick to compare and criticize —it also means positively that the members are to encourage each other, to love one another with the love like the love of Jesus Christ who died on the cross for us. As Christians we do not necessarily have to like every person, but we do have to love every person. This love is the New Testament kind of love. This love is not filial or erotic, but it is the brand-new kind of love of the New Testament. This is the love where we try to put ourselves in the other person's place and seek the best for the other person.

Isaiah walked with kings. One day this princely prophet was given the vision of the ideal fellowship. In Isaiah 41:6, God describes his dynamic group of people by saying, "They helped every one his neighbour; and every one said to his brother, Be of good courage."

God goes on to say concerning this cooperating group of people, "I have chosen thee and not cast you away. Fear thou not; for I am with thee: be not dismayed; for I am thy God: I will strengthen thee; I will help thee" (vv. 9-10). Here is the secret of the divinely chosen and divinely strengthened church: the members love the Lord, they love one another, and they encourage one another in the work of the Lord.

The Sun Belt is growing faster than any other section of the nation! Prospects unlimited have exploded all around us! This is the day, and now is the hour for the church to go forward for Christ! Bold Mission takes on hands and feet and achieves victories as we lead people to Christ in our church, in our nation, and in our world!

All through the history of Israel there were the three basic elements: the camp, the world around, and the small expeditionary force that led the congregation to go forward. Israel began its national existence as a camp: a poor, pitiful, handful of nomads huddled in the desert for protection. The camp always meant two things for Israel: a sacred place and a safe place. The camp was so sacred that the offering for sin was made outside the encampment. Look at Leviticus 9:1-2: "And it came to pass on the eighth day, that Moses called Aaron and his sons, and the elders of Israel; And he said unto Aaron, Take thee a young calf for a sin offering, and a ram for a burnt offering, without blemish, and offer them before the Lord." "The flesh and the hide he burnt with fire without the camp" (v. 11).

The camp was also the place for safety. Neither wild animals nor wild enemies could capture the people inside the camp. Guards surrounded them on either side. Each time the camp had to be moved, armed men went before and behind them for protection. Yes, always in the history of Israel there was this sacred and safe camp.

Now if the camp influenced the history of Israel, so did the world around. Whether they were friends and intermarried with the Israelites or whether they were enemies and sought to kill them, the people around had a powerful influence on the Hebrews. The pagan gods, the gross immorality, and the crushing injustice of their neighbors seeped into the lives of the Jews and poisoned their happiness. The Israelites became not only in the world but also of the world. Jeremiah's speech for God has become famous: "Hath a nation changed their gods, which are yet no gods? but my people have changed their glory for that which doth not profit. . . . My people have committed two evils; they have forsaken me the fountain of living waters, and hewed them out cisterns, broken cisterns, that can hold no water" (2:11-13).

The camp, the world around, and a redemptive expeditionary

force—always there was the tiny group of people with vision, the forward few, that prodded them out of their lethargy and stabbed them out of their sleep with the dynamic "thus saith the Lord" and led them out to follow God's will. Think of Joshua and Caleb. Consider Gideon and others, ready to sacrifice, ready to go, ready to serve the Lord!

Isn't this a striking picture of the need of the churches today? For many people the church is the camp, the sacred place, and the safe place. Certainly, the church is a sacred place. You can pray to God in other places; you can feel his presence in times of danger and distress; but somehow when you meet in the church with fellow Christians, sing the songs of Zion, search God's word in the Scriptures, and think his thoughts after him you know you are in a holy atmosphere.

The church is also the safe place. Here you are in little physical or emotional danger. The air is peaceful, the music is lovely, and the feeling of security and safety is yours just for entering the doors.

But the church must never be so sacred that we forget to give a welcome to the stranger in our midst. It must never be so sacred that we neglect a kind word and a friendly smile.

There is also danger in the safety of the church. A comfortable religion is a dangerous religion. It calls for compromises; it dilutes the gospel into a weak lemonade; it makes Christianity into a sham and a pretense. The religion of Jesus Christ is not a mathematical formula where you multiply, divide, add, and subtract, and always get the same answer. The religion of Jesus Christ is the dynamic discovery of a Friend; there are always new depths to be fathomed, new insights to be gained, and new horizons to be conquered! You are not invited to enjoy a plush velvet chair where you can be "at ease in Zion"; you are challenged to walk hand in hand with Christ who requires your last full measure of devotion and dedication and obedience!

The church is certainly the camp, and we also have the world around. Our grandfathers called it worldliness; today we call it secularism or humanism. Did you know that humanism has been recognized by the courts, even the Supreme Court, as a religion in this country? The sin of secularism or humanism is not simply doing this or that in the world; it is a subtle menace that creeps into our thinking when we least expect it. "The weather's too hot today to go to church." "I stayed out too late last night and need sleep." "I've been working too hard all week, need to rest, and stay home from church." Secularism is giving priority to the things of this world rather than the things of God. With these pitiful excuses many people fail to come to God's house, fail to study his Word, and fail to give their witness to people who look for guidance.

David Brainerd, who at the cost of his life carried the gospel to the American Indians, had the right attitude toward the things of this world. Listen to his private journal for April 25, 1742. "Farewell, vain world, my soul can bid you adieu; my Savior taught me to abandon you. Forbear to entice, cease then my soul to call; tis fixed through grace—my God shall be my all!" Christians must live in this world, but they must remain unaccommodated and unsoiled by the world. Paul says that we are not called to be conformed to this world, but we are called to transform the world.

The camp, the world around, and Christians too must have the expeditionary force. Christians must march forward outside the camp to reach people, singing the songs of Zion, carrying the sword of the Spirit, and blazing the banner of God across the blight of this world. The Hebrews, the early Christians, Luther and the reformers, Francis and his brothers, Wesley and the Methodists, Calvin and the Presbyterians, Truett and the Baptists—all suffered without the camp, giving their life blood that the Word of God might be proclaimed, and people won to Christ!

Ringing down through the centuries comes the clarion call to you and me of Hebrews 13:12, "Wherefore Jesus also, that he might sanctify the people with his own blood, suffered without the gate. Let us go forth therefore unto him without the camp." Bold Mission springs alive as Christians today go forward without the camp to win the lost, care for the unlovely, crash through the gates of secularism, and build Christ's kingdom that shall never end! Let us sing with Daniel W. Whittle:

> There's a royal banner given for display
>> To the soldiers of the King;
> As an ensign fair we lift it up today,
>> While as ransomed ones we sing.
> Marching on, marching on,
>> For Christ count ev'rything but loss!
> And to crown him King, toil and sing
>> 'Neath the banner of the cross!

9

The Church Is for the Unraveled
and Undone

Matthew 6:19 to 7:12; Isaiah 6

It was a beautiful autumn day in the city of Bern, Norway. Ten Norweigan patriots marched into the city square. Mothers and wives wept as the German capters lined their men up before the firing squad. Then came the roll of drums and the command, "Ready!"

Suddenly the assembled group began to sing the Norweigan national anthem. Through his tears, each Norweigan smiled for the pride of his country. The next command followed: "Aim - Fire!" The rifles cracked, and ten Norweigans fell to the dust with a song on their lips and a cause in their hearts! Each man who died had an undivided allegiance to his country.

A few months earlier a similar scene occurred in the area of Alsace, France. Five Frenchmen were lined up along the wall of a concentration camp. Each man was blindfolded. There came the roll of drums and the commands, "Ready - Aim - Fire!" As the rifles cracked, a shout rang out from those Frenchmen which echoed throughout the hills of their homeland, "Vive la France!" "Long live France!" Each man paid for his allegiance with his life!

Many years earlier, a little country was born across the seas. Older republics chuckled to think that this little country called the United States dreamed of becoming a great nation, yet a few men of vision believed in that dream. Then one day in a town along the Atlantic coastline of America, a crowd assembled to watch the hanging of a young man. This patriot's name was

Nathan Hale. Just before they strung him to the gallows, they asked if he had anything to say. "Yes," said Hale. "I only regret that I have but one life to lose for my country." A man with an undivided allegiance.

Many years before these incidents, another man died for a different kind of Kingdom. It is not a kingdom that you can see with your eyes or touch with your hands but a kingdom that is much more real.

It all happened just outside the city walls of Jerusalem. Stephen was speaking to a multitude of Jews and telling them about the kingdom of God. He told them that they must believe in Jesus as the Christ in order to enter that kingdom, but they gnashed their teeth, cried with a loud voice, drug him out of the city, and began to stone him. Looking steadfastly up into heaven, Stephen prayed, "Lord Jesus, receive my spirit" (Acts 7:59). Then "he kneeled down, and cried with a voice, Lord, lay not this sin to their charge. And when he had said this, he fell asleep" (v. 60). Stephen had displayed his allegiance with the sacrifice of his life! This demonstration of loyalty was so appealing, so attracting to the brilliant Paul standing nearby, that it gave a traumatic demonstration of a man's loyalty to Christ, and it excited the conscience of Paul so that he later became convicted, giving his life to Christ to become one of the most dynamic missionaries the world has ever seen.

Today we are inspired to analyze Jesus' command for absolute allegiance to the kingdom of God. He makes this demand by describing two parables. To begin, we notice the parable of dividing allegiance with earthly possessions. The first earthly possession is the parable of the divided mind. Look at Matthew 6 "Lay not up for yourselves treasures upon earth, where moth and rust doth corrupt, and where thieves break through and steal: But lay up for yourselves treasures in heaven, where neither moth nor rust doth corrupt, and where thieves do not break through nor steal: For where your treasure is, there will your heart be also" (vv. 19-21).

This is the parable of the divided mind. The heart means the whole personality of a person. The Hebrew philosophy thought of the heart as being the seat of one's responses to the challenges of life. As Dr. Edward McDowell taught in his New Testament classes at Southern Baptist Theological Seminary, "If you follow the teachings of the Sermon on the Mount, you won't go crazy! You will have mental, emotional, and spiritual health if you live by the principles and practices of the kingdom of God." John M. Moore wrote:

> This is the church of my dreams,
> A church adequate for the task,
> The church of the warm heart,
> Of the open mind,
> Of the adventurous spirit,
> The church that cares,
> A working church,
> A winsome church,
> A winning church,
> This is the church of my dreams,
> The church of the Living God!

Suppose someone asked you, "What is your dream church?" What would you say? Suppose your imagination could soar through the stars and fathom the deepest yearnings of the human heart, how would you fashion your dream church? Perhaps Moore's words suggest a starting point when he says, "It is a working church, a winsome church, and a winning church."

Christ Jesus, the chief corner stone, said, "My Father worketh hitherto, and I work" (John 5:17). A lady recently went into a variety store searching for a compass. "We have a compass for making circles," the clerk explained, "but not for going places."

The church of Jesus Christ is never to be simply an instrument for running around in circles; she is God's divine instrument for going places, for action, and for definite arrival at definite goals. As Maltbie Babcock has penned,

> We are not here to dream, to drift,
> We have jobs to do and loads to lift,
> Shun not the struggle - face it,
> 'Tis God's gift.

The church of Jesus Christ gives us the opportunity to demonstrate our loyalty by our work. In the church we say that we study the Word of God. Christ demands that both the teaching and the learning be put into practice. In the church we claim to be growing in Christian maturity. Does anyone in anyplace ever grow without work? Christ invited James and John: "Come ye after me, and I shall make you to become fishers of men" (Mark 1:17). Christians are always in a state of "becoming," becoming more mature Christians. We are saved by one complete and irrevocable decision to give our lives to Christ, but we become mature, loyal Christians only by hundreds of day-by-day decisions and deeds. We must work at this business of becoming "more like the Master."

A lady was watching a potter at his work. One foot with regular speed turned the wheel while the other foot rested patiently on the ground.

The lady said sympathetically, "How tired that working foot must get!"

Raising his eyes the old potter explained, "No, Ma'am; it isn't the foot that works that gets tired: its the foot that stands."

The church offers us the opportunity of demonstrating our

loyalty by working and producing a winsome church. A certain man who for many years had been indifferent to any church has now become an active member of his Sunday School class. He explained, "A friend insisted that I visit in his class, and I came just to shut him up. But when I attended I found that you could feel that the class was alive and working. I was attracted by the men's enthusiasm and loyalty in the Master's service, and now its Sunday School every Sunday!"

Your church gives you the opportunity to demonstrate your loyalty by working and winning. Your church is deeply concerned about winning people to Christ.

Amid the downtown district of a large city stands an historic old church. Her outside walls are heavily coated with the dust and grime of the crowded streets. The entire church might easily be passed by as of no particular interest except for the light that comes streaming through the stained-glass windows. Forbidding and aloof during the day, the church becomes alive and beckoning to people at night. The change happens because of the life within. It is the light within that gives the church her impelling invitation.

Christ said, "I am the light of the world" (John 8:12), and the Christian demonstrates his or her loyalty to Christ by helping people along the path to the eternal Light.

Certain people came to the disciples in the long ago and said, "Sir, we would see Jesus" (John 12:21). This is still the compelling cry that leaps from hungry hearts in every city in America: "We want to see Jesus, we must see Jesus!"

What about that person who works by your side in the office, the shop, or the factory? Maybe she is a neighbor that lives two houses across the way. Perhaps he has been playing basketball or attending class with you all week. Have you remembered this is a person Christ loves? Have you asked whether this person is a Christian? Have you prayed that this person may come face-to-face with the Savior?

Near the entrance to the corridor of the world-famous Johns Hopkins Hospital in Baltimore stands a gigantic figure of Christ carved in marble. A look of tender sympathy and solicitation shines from the Master's face, and his arms are extended as if welcoming the multitudes. On the base of the pedestal is inscribed his own invitation: "Come unto me, all ye that labour and are heavy laden, and I will give you rest" (Matt. 11:28). Experienced nurses tell how many a weary soul, worried with sickness or sin, has gazed at that statue and surrendered to the Savior. "Yes," smiled a nurse, "the restoration and reinforcement that comes to a person when he comes to Christ are really inspiring and wonderful!"

Several years ago a Baptist deacon was walking along the river warf in a large city when he saw a pair of worn-out shoes sticking out from under a warf barrel. The shoes reflected the other rags that covered the tousle-haired boy. But the deacon saw more than just ragged shoes and ragged clothes. He saw a boy for whom Christ died, and whom Christ wanted to lead to newness of life, and the deacon led Russell Conwell to Christ.

During his lifetime, Russell became so possessed by Christ that he founded the Grace Temple Baptist Church, Temple University, Temple University Hospital, and he became the number-one citizen of Philadelphia! Yes, something wonderful happens in a person's life when he opens his heart to him who is the light of Life, and each Christian is challenged in these days to show his or her loyalty to Christ by leading people to the Master.

The Master was teaching a group of people one day when a rich young ruler joined the crowd. "Good Master, what good thing shall I do, that I may have eternal life?" (Matt. 19:16).

Jesus answered, "Why callest thou me good? there is none

good but one, that is, God: . . . If thou wilt be perfect, go and sell that thou hast, and give to the poor, . . . and come follow me" (19:17-21).

The man went away completely characterized by sorrow, for he was possessed by many possessions. What was Jesus asking the young man to do? The Master was asking him to change banks. He was asking this man to put his treasure in heaven instead of on earth where it will perish. He was asking the young man to have singleness of mind and heart, so his loyalty would be undivided toward the kingdom of God.

The teachings we notice in Matthew 6 and 7 are concerned with divided purposes. The purpose to which your life is committed will determine your action day by day. You cannot have a pagan purpose and create a Christian character. The Scripture reads, "The eye is the lamp of the body. So, if your eye is sound, your whole body will be full of light. . . . If then the light in you is darkness, how great is the darkness!" (6:22-23, RSV).

There are paradox of the divided mind and the paradox of the divided purpose. The Bible also warns us against the peril of divided service. "No man can serve two masters: for either he will hate the one, and love the other; or else he will hold to the one, and despise the other. Ye cannot serve God and mammon" (6:24). This is one of the most-quoted passages in the Sermon on the Mount, and its truth should be written indelibly on the heart of every Christian. We must constantly bend our wills to God's will.

This leads us to Jesus' demand for supreme and complete loyalty. "But seek ye first the kingdom of God, and his righteousness; and all these things shall be added unto you" (6:33).

Christ does not make a long list of little demands upon our lives but one supreme demand that coordinates and organizes the total direction of our lives. Christ says that we are to put him and his kingdom first.

The apostle Paul was inspired by Christ to write, "This one thing I do [not a dozen, not six, not two], forgetting those things which are behind, and reaching forth unto those things which are before, I press toward the mark for the prize of the high calling of God in Christ Jesus" (Phil. 3:13-14).

Savonarola was one of the greatest preachers that Italy has ever produced. He preached with such conviction that the entire city of Florence, Italy, began to repent. But Savonarola denounced the immoral and wicked leaders. They stirred up the people against the preacher, and he was cruelly tortured and condemned to death by fire. They led him out before the yelling, jeering mob and prepared to burn him.

But Savonarola stood erect and declared, "You may burn me alive, if you will, but you can never, never snatch the living Christ out of my heart!"

Does Jesus Christ mean something to you? Does Jesus Christ mean everything to you? If so, will you witness boldly for him?

10

The Bothered and Bewildered Are Transformed into Biblical Witnesses

2 Corinthians 5:14-22

Sören Kierkegaard related an interesting story that has become a parable for our times. One of the most beloved and most thrilling phenomena in Europe is the Touring Circus. They parade through the large towns and the small towns bringing poetry and popcorn to many people!

One day, a relatively small circus had just pitched it's camp near Copenhagen when suddenly the main tent caught fire. The clown was the only one appropriately attired, and he rushed into the city to plead with the people to come and help the circus people put out the fire. The city people looked at his strange makeup, his long funny nose, his comical clothes, and they would not believe him. No one lifted a finger or walked a foot to help him put out the fire. It was not until they lifted their eyes and began to see the red flames on the horizon that the people were willing to go out and extinquish the blaze. At last they realized that this was not merely a clown: he was a person to be helped and to be encouraged, a real person with urgent and important needs.

One New Testament scholar maintains that the difference between the early church and the church today is that the early church was power conscious, and the modern church is problem conscious. Like many of our clever sayings, this statement has an element of truth, but we need to probe a little deeper. We need to recognize that the early church had her problems, perhaps that this very point of seeing people as they really were rather than as they appeared.

In the sixth and seventh chapters of Acts we find a problem that could have really rocked the church, the problem of the distribution of funds to the needy. But the disciples began the problem solving by prayer, faced each other in an atmosphere of trust, earnestly enlisted the leadership of God's Holy Spirit, and the problem was solved. How many obstacles and objections could be overcome, how many heartaches and hurts could be healed today if we would prayerfully seek the fresh insight of God's Holy Spirit, search our own hearts, and witness to people of Christ.

It is easy to give lip service to loving the whole world, but it is not always easy to love that individual person who may make it difficult to be loved.

Dr. Paul Rees gave a series of Bible lectures at the Chattanooga Bible Institute that brought many people face-to-face with this problem. He reminded us of these searching words in 2 Corinthians 5, "For we must all appear before the judgment seat of Christ; . . . Knowing therefore the terror of the Lord, we persuade men; . . . Now then we are ambassadors for Christ, . . . we pray you in Christ's stead, be ye reconciled to God."

Since we have been reconciled to God by Christ Jesus, we are called by God to be reconcilers, ambassadors for Christ, to seek to bring men and women, boys and girls, first to Christ, then to one another in loyalty and uplifting love.

We have so many people today who are eager to analyze and evaluate other people's problems, but they do not wish to bother about the people themselves. Today we need to see people as Christ sees people, with their wishful longings, worries, warts, and all, and to witness to the people of Christ.

In Paris during the Middle Ages most of the educated people spoke Latin, and the uneducated people spoke the barbarian tongues of the northern Europeans. Two young doctors in a hospital in Paris had a man brought in who looked just like a beggar. Actually, he was a scholar who had taken the vows of poverty and had been overcome by heat exhaustion. These two young doctors, thinking that he would not understand them because they spoke in Latin, reasoned that he was not long for this world anyhow as he was just skin and bones. One said to the other, "You know that experiment that we have wanted to try on somebody, why don't we attempt it on this worthless wretch?"

The genuine scholar opened his eyes and in flawless Latin asked, "Would you call any man worthless whom Jesus loves and for whom Jesus died?"

Do we see people in the city, the suburb, and the country through the eyes of Christ? Do we realize that each person is an immortal soul whom Christ loves and for whom Christ died? Are we motivated to go and lead people to Christ today?

If you make a critical examination of the Scriptures in the light of current needs, you will discover that in difficult times there were four key cities in Asia—Laodicea, Colosse, Hierapolis, and Philadelphia—much like Knoxville, Nashville, Memphis, and Chattanooga, Tennessee, today.

Laodicea was surrounded by the snow-capped mountain range of the Cademus, and it had surged to importance under the imperial rule. It was famous for raising an unusual breed of sheep and manufacturing an eye salve called "Phrygian powder."

To the right of Laodicea was located the sprawling city of Hierapolis. Epictetus, the noble Stoic teacher, was born in this famous manufacturing city, famous for dyeing wool in scarlet and purple.

Between Laodicea and Hierapolis, there stood the thriving city of Colosse, and north Colosse was the exciting word-keeping city of Philadelphia. All four cities shared in a prosperous outlook.

Epaphras, a most successful businessman, was born and reared in Colosse. When he confronted Christ, when his heart was warmed by the love of God and his soul was stirred by the Spirit of God, he committed his life to Christ, and he initiated several New Testament churches in all four cities of this ancient, urban megalopolis. Naturally, Paul and Epaphras became close friends, and Paul wrote his letter to the Colossians to challenge the people of these four exciting cities to arrange their lives around the redemptive Christ. No greater concepts or grander language is found anywhere in the Scriptures than in Paul's letter to the Colossians.

You can imagine your city as being typical of one of these ancient cities. As we read the Word of God as it is recorded in Paul's letter to the Colossians, imagine that Paul is writing to you and your city. "To the saints and faithful brethren in Christ which are at Colosse: . . . We give thanks to God and the Father of our Lord Jesus Christ, . . . who hath delivered us from the power of darkness, and hath translated us into the kingdom of his dear Son: In whom we have redemption through his blood, even the forgiveness of sins: . . . by him were all things created, . . . and by him all things consist" (Col. 1:2-17).

What a tremendous and exciting concept! Christ is the Creator of all things in heaven and in earth, visible and invisible; and Christ is the sovereign Lord over all people, principalities, and powers! Evangelism is born in the lordship of Christ!

Today, instead of sort of patronizing God by thinking how lucky God is to have affluent little us on his side, we need to go to our knees and humbly acknowledge Christ's authorship of all our blessings and Christ's lordship of all our lives! Then, we need to arise from our prayers to get busy leading people who are pouring into our cities from all directions to the foot of the Cross and to the heart of the living Christ! The blasé, sophisticated, surging, sprawling city is not only where the action is but also the place where hearts are yearning—minds are searching—to apprehend and to be apprehended by the thrilling Christ and by his love. Christ died for the people in the country, for the people in the suburbs, and for the people in the city; and today Christ calls us not to be discouraged, not to be disappointed but to be dynamically dedicated, and to do our part to lead people everywhere to the redeeming Christ.

Not long ago a druggist with whom I had become acquainted had a son who started attending our Sunday School. The mother and father lived outside the city in the country and went to a church of another denomination, but as the boy kept coming regularly to our church the day came when he said he wanted to join our Baptist church.

The father told his son it would be all right for him to join the Baptist church, and when the father and the son came down the aisle we welcomed them. The father leaned forward and said that he would like to join our church along with his son.

Two Sundays later we had planned to have a baptismal service in the evening worship hour. That Sunday afternoon a telephone call came from the druggist: "My friend, you wouldn't want a man to join your church who is not a Christian, would you?"

I replied, "No, Fred, but perhaps we need to talk about it. I'll come over to your drugstore, and we can explore this possibility."

It was Sunday afternoon in a crowded drugstore in the heart of town. People were milling about, buying cosmetics, and getting prescriptions filled. There was no alternative except to talk behind the prescription counter. I explained to Fred how he could put his name and his life into John 3:16 so that it would read, "For God so loved Fred, that he gave his only begotten Son, that when Fred believed in him, Fred would not perish, but have everlasting life."

When asked if he would like to make this decision to give his life to Christ, Fred answered, "Yes, I would."

We agreed to share a prayer right there in the midst of the rush and rumble of the busy drugstore. Fred agreed for me to say a phrase or a sentence, then he would repeat the phrase in his prayer of commitment unto God. We went through the prayer of thanking God for sending Christ and of thanking Christ for offering us salvation. Then I prayed and suggested to him, "And now, O Lord, I give my life to Christ to live for him from this time and forever." Fred prayed those words, then, before I could say Amen he added, "And thank you so much, O God, for sending my friend here to our drugstore to help me give my life to Christ."

Yes, for the people in the country, in the suburbs, and the inner city, there is not another name given from heaven among men whereby we must be saved but the name of Jesus, and we need to give Christ all the credit as we seek to lead people to him.

The duke of Wellington has been called the toughest commander in the British army. One day a young man asked, "Sir, what do you think about our pastor's emphasis upon every man being a personal witness for Christ?" The iron duke replied, "Young man, look to your marching orders."

What are the marching orders for Christians, for the soldiers of the Cross? The real Christian has one Commander: Jesus Christ. He has one weapon: the Word of God. He has one armor: righteousness. He has one power: the Holy Spirit. He has one battlefield the entire universe. He has one objective: the souls of men, "For the kingdoms of this world once become the kingdoms of our Lord, and of his Christ; and he shall reign for ever and ever" (Rev. 11:15).

Return with me to a day when Christ was on earth in the flesh. He had been crucified, and he had risen from the grave. Just before he ascended into heaven, what would be his last command to his soldiers? What would be his final words before he went to be with his Father? In Acts 1:6-8, we have this scene depicted: "When they therefore were come together, they asked of him saying, Lord, wilt thou at this time restore again the kingdom to Israel?"

"And he said unto them, it is not for you to know the times or the seasons, which the Father hath put in his own power. But ye shall receive power, after the Holy Ghost is come upon you: and ye shall be witnesses unto me both in Jerusalem, and in all Judaea, and in Samaria, and unto the uttermost part of the earth."

Why did Jesus specifically mention that we are to witness in these places? What is significant about each one? Let us take them in reverse order for emphasis.

Jesus broadens our horizons and lifts up our eyes to genuinely look upon the fields as he says, "Ye shall receive power, after that the Holy Ghost is come upon you: and ye shall be witnesses unto me . . . unto the uttermost parts of the earth." Dr. Baker James Cauthen often said, "God is able to do more in our generation than we have dared to ask or think! It is time we realized the urgency and necessity of world missions." If we are going to win the world for Christ, we have only this generation with which to do it! God is ready, eager, and able to bless our efforts to win the peoples of the world to Christ. Today is the day for us to pray and give sacrificially and go to share the good news to all the world.

Jesus also said you shall witness unto me in Judaea and Samaria. To us today Judaea and Samaria would mean the other states here in our United States. Deep in our hearts and throbbing in our brains we must be home-missionary minded.

We must do our utmost to bring the people of our nation to the foot of the cross and to a vital encounter with Christ.

Third, Jesus tells us where we should begin, "Ye shall be witnesses unto me in Jerusalem." To every Christian, Jerusalem means our spiritual hometown. We as Christians ought to witness for Christ right where we live. Bishop Arthur Moore told about preaching a revival in a small town in Georgia. One day they went to visit the man who was called the roughest, toughest man in town. They shared with him how to become a Christian, and that night when the invitation was given, this rough, unshaven man rushed down the aisle, threw his arms around the preacher, and hugged him as he gave his life to Christ.

Several years later, Bishop Moore was passing through that same town, and he stopped in a hotel for dinner. After the meal he received a check marked "Paid in full." He then discovered that the manager of the hotel was named Arthur Moore Smith. He was the son of the rough man who had formerly been won to Christ, and the man had named his son after Bishop Moore. The son commented, "Sir, my father became a fine, respected Christian witness right here in our hometown when Christ came into his heart."

Christian empathy, Christian concern, Christian love is what we need to move us to witness for Christ. In Romans 5:8 we read, "But God commendeth his love toward us, in that, while we were yet sinners, Christ died for us."

How can you blacken the barren bleakness of breaking the will of God? How can you show the criminal contentions that creep into the chasm of men's minds and cause us to sin? Is there a word hideous enough to describe it? Is there a thought dark enough to paint the rebellion of man? Paradoxical though it may seem, sin in its unctuous ugliness can only be apprehended against the love of God. Even while we were yet sinners God loved us, and it is only as we comprehend that love of God that we become conscious of the awfulness of sin.

John 3:16 begins, "For God so loved the world, that he gave his only begotten Son." People may argue about the meaning of justification; people may struggle with the meaning of sanctification; people may fight over the implications of regeneration, but when they speak of the love of God they burst forth in singing the Doxology! "Praise God, from whom all blessings flow!"

Did you ever wonder why the multitudes followed Jesus? When the disciples went out preaching the good news, why did pagan men and women believe? When the apostle Paul went to a small town and preached only two or three days, how was he able to leave a church in their midst? Because Jesus brought the love of God to all humanity! Pagan gods were gods to fear, but Jesus brought the good news of the love of God. Does God love a tax collector? Yes! Does God love the unlovable? Yes! Does God really love the sinner? Yes! God is not a God of fear but the God of love.

It was a dark night in the country of Judea. Shepherds were tending their flocks along the hillside, and suddenly there came a blinding flash: the angel of the Lord stood beside them! They were greatly afraid. Fear possessed them, but the angel spoke words of comfort, "Fear not: for, behold, I bring you good tidings of great joy, which shall be to all people. For unto you is born this day in the city of David a Saviour, which is Christ the Lord" (Luke 2:10-11). The plea of hungry hearts everywhere has been answered decisively and dynamically in God's Son! The God who speaks and worlds come into being, the God who sighs and whole nations are wiped off the face of the earth, the God who smiles and a little child is born—this great God has come into this world to share his love in his Son, Christ Jesus.

It was a cold gray dawn in the little area of Galilee. Two strong, stalwart men stood and gazed out across the sea. The stronger spoke, "Simon, . . . lovest thou me?" (John 21:15-17).

"Yea, Lord; thou knowest that I love thee." "Feed my lambs."

"Simon, son of Jonas, lovest thou me?"

"Lord, thou knowest all things; thou knowest that I love thee."

"Feed my sheep."

If we really love Jesus, then we'll care for the people who are in need, love the unlovely, be concerned about the lost, and lead people to the One who is "the way, the truth, and the life" (John 14:6).

In a large metropolitan area there was a tiny mission church. Into that church came all types of men, but there was one particular man, an old major, who came every Sunday. Everyone knew why he came. The mission had the custom of giving everyone who professed Christ as Savior a room for the night and the accompanying meals. The old major was possessed by alcohol; so he came every Sunday, made his profession, and received a room with the meals.

The pastor and the board of deacons pondered over the problem and decided to fix him. The next Sunday came, and, surely enough, there was the old major marching down the aisle. Just as he reached two rows from the front, three deacons grabbed him, took him to the back of the church, and threw him out in the street!

That night the minister had trouble going to sleep. He knew he had been just, but something was wrong. He arose and searched up and down the alleys, the bars, the saloons until, finally, he found the old major in a back alley. He lifted him up, "I'm sorry we threw you out. If you come back, we'll give you the room with the meals. I love you."

Suddenly it seemed as if the haze passed from the old major's face. "What's that you say?"

"I said, 'I'm sorry we threw you out.' "

"No, that's not it."

"I said, If you'll come back, we'll give you the room and the meals.' "

"No, that's not it."

"I said, 'I love you.' " "You know," said the old major, "no one has ever said that to me before."

The old major became a powerful witness for Christ right there in his community. Why? Because someone shared with him the uplifting and redeeming love of God in Christ Jesus.

With people who have been born again, a church becomes a forceful catalyst in today's world.

11

The Disciplined Congregation
Is a Divine Catalyst
Philippians 2:5-11

One of the deepest problems of today is that we folks do not know the Bible as well as we should. J. P. McGraw of North Augusta, South Carolina, tells this true story that happened in northern Arkansas. A lawyer reported that one of his colleagues kept winning case after case by quoting the Bible. He would preface his remarks by saying "As the Bible says," or, "As the Word of God declares," and he would come out with a statement that exactly proved his point. Over and over this lawyer kept winning his cases, so finally another lawyer became jealous and decided to challenge him.

One day they were standing around in the courtroom, and the second lawyer challenged, "You're always pretending to quote the Bible to prove your point. I don't believe you know the Bible that well. In fact, I will bet you five dollars that you can't quote the Lord's Prayer!" The first lawyer was put on the spot, and he had to do something.

Without cracking a smile or looking to the right or left, the lawyer bowed his head looking very sanctimonious as he began, "Now I lay me down to sleep. I pray the Lord my soul to keep," and so on to the end of the little child's prayer. The remarkable thing was that the lawyer who had challenged him exclaimed, "Well, go ahead and keep the money! You *did* know the Bible after all!"

The Bible abounds in notes of rejoicing, rejoicing that the

·Christian can succeed and sacrifice and serve for the sake of Christ!

In Acts 5:41 we read, "They departed from the presence of the council, rejoicing that they were counted worthy to suffer shame for his name." All through his Word God stipulates that burdens can be borne with rejoicing, loneliness can be dispelled with love, worry can be conquered with revival if Christians are willing to hold forth the Word of life and make sacrifices for Christ, accepting Christian discipline in this dangerous and disturbing world.

In many churches of my denomination, September is designated as the month of the church. The Bible abounds in striking images of the church. In a moment of inspiration John called the church, "the bride of Christ" (Rev. 21:9-10), and Paul saw the church as "the body of Christ" (1 Cor. 12:27).

Dr. Arthur Moore says succinctly, "I am convinced that what our distraught and distressed world seeks is not a new definition of religion but a new realization of Christ's power, not a speculation about the church but the spectacle of a church reborn, passionately seeking to know and to do the will of God."

When Paul called the church "the body of Christ," it must have seemed like a significant name for a very insignificant group of people. There were few if any really commanding personalities. They were fumbling, fallible, blundering men and women, boys and girls; but they had Christ as their Savior, Christ as their Master, Christ as their Shepherd. They could read it in each other's eyes; they could feel it in every heart-throb, and God riveted this most unlikely looking group of people into being the magnificent body of Christ upon this earth!

As the ancient preacher said in his quaint way, "A body without a spirit is a corpse, and a spirit without a body is a ghost!" The church of the 1980s has the high and holy commission of being the body of Christ, the agent through whom Christ continues all those ministries he began to do while physically present here on earth. To make this impact, each member of the church must not only accept but welcome discipline.

First of all, we need the discipline of recognizing that we worship the one true, all-powerful God of the universe. In spite of the impact of all the materialistic inflationary pressures of these days, in spite of the problems of poverty, pollution, and overpopulation, church members today must be bold to declare that the living God is real; and that this great and glorious God has come to live among us in Christ Jesus with hope in his eyes, healing in his hands, and an irresistible love in his heart.

Inspired by Christ the church membership boldly declares that our God is not a spectator but a participant in life's struggles, that life itself is not some endless, reasonless ebb and flow. God knows the way of our pilgrimage, and God cares about the way that we walk this road. God's children have their faces toward the dawning of that fadeless day; and someday soon, at noontime, or in the world's late evening, Christ and Christ's church will win through completely, and every knee shall bow, and every tongue confess that Jesus Christ is Lord.

Diotrephes was the disgruntled man who wanted to have his way in all the activities of the church. He styled himself the chief backbiter, and he was always stirring up trouble, always insisting that his demands were inspired. If the people did not go along, he growled and grumbled about it. Dr. W. O. Carver, professor of missions at Southern Baptist Theological Seminary, often counseled, "Let's all read about Diotrephes in the third Letter of John and vow never to be like him!" All troublemakers are displaced persons in the church of Jesus Christ. The church must be united and disciplined as never before to proclaim the divine sovereignty of God and to practice Christlikeness. The church of Jesus Christ is never a rest home for celebrated saints, as one scholar said. The church is a hospital of struggling sinners who are striving to get healing and to grow more like Jesus!

Today as never before church members need to pray, "O God, our Father, we pray that thou wilt give us an insight into the amazing, kind, and merciful heart of Jesus Christ that you through Christ may possess our minds and hearts." The Japanese translation of Philippians 2:5 is, "Let beat within you the same heart that beat within Christ Jesus."

Dr. G. K. Ober of Princeton writes, "A few years ago, I had a dream. In my dream five men stood on a hillside and gazed out across the lake of Galilee. Peter, Andrew, Matthew, John, and Paul met twenty years after Pentecost to discuss the crises in their lives. Peter was having trouble supporting his family; Matthew had an offer of a large salary with great fringe benefits to return to his tax-collecting business; Paul had lost all his possessions.

"As usual Peter opened the discussion. 'My mother-in-law has started a boardinghouse in Capernaum, and it won't cost us too much to live there while I get reestablished in the fishing business. I can make a good living fishing all week, and on Sunday I'll have time for a few revivals in the little towns around the lake.'

"Matthew explained, 'I have an exciting offer with a huge salary and fringe benefits to return to the customs house. This just may be an offer I cannot turn down!'

"Paul explained, 'Aquila and Priscilla have hit it big in the tent-making business in Ephesus, and they want me to open a branch office in Philippi. I can make tents during the week, do some evangelistic work on Sunday, and lay by some money for a rainy day.'

"Then old Andrew interrupted them with the question,

'Peter, do you remember the day when we thought you'd lost your mother-in-law? She didn't seem to have a chance to live, but Christ came, and Christ made her well! Take a closer look at this lake. Here Christ gave us the miraculous haul of fish and that miraculous challenge as he said, 'Fear not, from henceforth I will make you to become fishers of men.' Remember the look of longing on Jesus' face when he asked us to pray that more laborers would be sent forth into the harvest? If we are going to pray that other men and women will rise up and follow Christ, how can we do less?

"John, who was leaning on Peter's shoulder, felt a tear drop on his hand, and looking over to Paul he saw the old fire being rekindled in the apostle's face. 'Brethren, I think it's time to pray.'

"After the prayer, Paul said, 'Good-bye, my friends. I must catch the next boat to Ephesus. I'll get Aquila and Priscilla to put up the money for a revival in that old city that will shake the whole of Asia for Jesus Christ!'

" 'So long, boys,' said Peter, 'Andrew and I will just have time to say good-bye to the folks before we join the midnight caravan to Babylon (Iran). They need the gospel desperately over there!'

" 'Good-bye, boys,' said Matthew, 'I will get the other tax collectors to chip in and help me finance a five-year campaign for Christ in Egypt. Practically the whole country is eager to hear the good news of Jesus Christ!' "[1]

Perhaps the deepest need for the discipline of church members today is that we shall pause and discover the mind of Christ. Paul exclaims to his most-beloved Christian fellowship, the Philippians, in chapter 2: "Let this mind be in you, which was also in Christ Jesus: Who, being in the form of God, thought it not robbery to be equal with God: But made himself of no reputation, and took upon him the form of a servant,

. . . he humbled himself, and became obedient unto death, even the death of the cross. Wherefore God also hath highly exalted him, and given him a name which is above every name" (vv. 5-9).

Dr. Ray Frank Robbins has posed this question: "What do you think Paul meant by 'the mind of Christ?' Certainly he did not mean that we were to be as sharp as intellectually astute as Christ. We would never make it. Certainly, he did not mean that we would have all the knowledge of Christ because there is a sense in which as God is all-knowing, so Christ is omniscient."

The more we reflect upon this profound suggestion, the more we realize that the only way we can have the mind of Christ would be to have the same attitude of Christ—the same attitude toward God's will and toward people.

Christ is the perfect example of how Southern Baptists should act in the 1980s. He is the complete example of humility and self-sacrifice for the sake of others. Christ's attitude toward God and toward people was one of self-giving at whatever the cost. The proof of his attitude was his incarnation, his lowly service, his ignominious death. When Jesus chose to come upon this earth, he knew it would mean setting aside the regal splendor of his heavenly home, suffering the dense weight of your sins and mine; but love moved his heart, love made him man, and love won the victory!

Fulton Oursler tells us that Pete Richards was the loneliest man in town on the day Mary Grace came to the door of his shop. Pete's small business had come down to him from his grandfather. The little front window was strewn with the disarray of old-fashioned things: bracelets, lockets, gold rings, and silver boxes.

On this winter's afternoon a child was standing there, her forehead against the windowpane, studying each treasure as if she were looking for something special. Finally she straightened up and entered the store.

The shadowy interior of Pete Richard's establishment was even more cluttered than his show window. Behind the counter stood Pete himself, a man not more than thirty but with hair already turning gray. There was a forbidding air about him as he looked at his small customer.

"Mister," she began, "would you please let me look at that string of blue beads in the window?"

Pete parted the draperies and lifted out the lovely necklace. The turquoise stones gleamed brightly as he spread the ornament before her. "They're just perfect," smiled the child. "Will you please wrap them up real pretty for me?"

Pete studied her with a stony air. "Are you buying these for someone?"

"They're for my big sister. You see, this will be the first Christmas since Mother died. My sister takes care of me all year, and I've been looking for the most fabulous Christmas present for her! Now I've found it!"

"How much money do you have?" asked Pete impatiently. She had busily untied the knots in her handkerchief, and now she poured out a handful of pennies on the counter. "I emptied my bank," she explained simply.

Pete Richards looked at her thoughtfully. The trusting look in her blue eyes struck him like a stab of an old wound. "Just a minute," he said, and turned toward the back of the store. Over his shoulder he called, "What's your name?" as he quietly removed the price tag.

The little girl answered simply, "Mary Grace."

When Pete returned, the package lay in his hand wrapped in scarlet paper and tied with a green ribbon. "There," he said. "Don't lose it on the way home."

She thanked him and smiled happily over her shoulder as she

ran out the door. Through the window he watched her go while desolation flooded his soul. Something about Mary Grace and her string of beads had reached inside him and stirred a grief that would not stay buried. The child's hair was wheat yellow, her eyes sea blue; and once upon a time, not long before, Pete had been in love with a girl with hair the same yellow and with eyes just as blue. The same turquoise necklace was to have been hers, but there had come a rainy night—a truck skidding across a slippery road—and the life was crushed out of his sweetheart! Since then, Pete Richards had lived too much with his grief and solitude.

During the next ten days, trade was brisk. When the last customer had gone late on Christmas Eve, he sighed with relief; but for Pete Richards the night was not quite over. The door opened, and a young woman rushed in. Her hair was golden yellow, and her eyes were sea blue. Without speaking, she drew from her purse an object loosely wrapped in scarlet paper. Presently the string of blue beads lay gleaming again before him.

"Did this come from your shop?" she asked.

He answered softly, "Yes, it did."

"Are the stones real?"

"Yes. Not perhaps the finest quality, but very real."

"Can you remember to whom you sold them?"

"She was a small girl. Her name was Mary Grace. She bought them for her older sister as a Christmas present."

"How much are they worth?"

"The price," he told her simply, "is always a confidential matter between the seller and the customer."

"But Mary Grace has never had more than a few pennies of spending money. How could she pay for them?"

Pete was folding the colorful paper back into its creases,

rewrapping the little package neatly as before. "She paid the biggest price anyone can pay," he said. "She gave all she had."

A silence filled the little curio shop. In some faraway steeple, a bell began to peal. The little package lying on the counter, the question in the eyes of the beautiful girl, the strange feeling of renewal struggling unreasonably in the heart of this lonely man—all had come to be because of the love of a little child.

"But why did you do it?" she pleaded.

He held out the gift in his hand. "It's already Christmas morning," he said, "and it's my misfortune that I have no one to whom to give a present. Would you please let me see you home and wish you a Merry Christmas at your door?"

And so, to the pealing sound of many bells in the midst of many happy people, Pete Richards and a girl whose name he had yet to learn walked out into the beginning of a new relationship that is as old as humanity itself—the beginning of the great-giving day that makes the light of Christ's love burst through all the darkness of this world to break our hearts and mend them, to give us a new mind, a new attitude, a new heart, and a new love that we could never deserve: the Son of God's spirit of giving and loving and lifting![2]

NOTES

Introduction

1. John McClanahan, *1 Peter: The Message of Encouragement* (Nashville: Convention Press, 1962), p. 48.

Chapter 1

1. The idea for this discussion of personal encounter came from Professor James Stewart in a New Testament class at the University of Edinburgh in Scotland.

2. David Redding, *The Parables He Told* (New York: Harper, 1962), pp. 45 ff.

3. Much later this story became the foundation for the song, "Tie a Yellow Ribbon Round the Old Oak Tree."

Chapter 2

1. Some of these criticisms came from Ronald Sleeth, *Persuasive Preaching* (Berrien Springs, MI: Andrews University Press, 1981), pp. 78-80.

Chapter 5

1. Betty Malz, *Prayers That Are Answered* (Lincoln, VA: Chosen Books, 1980), pp. 65-68. Used by permission.

Chapter 11

1. The author has made every effort to locate the source of these quotations from G. K. Ober. He trusts that this acknowledgment is sufficient.